AI in Cybersecurity

Securing the Digital Frontier

Table of Contents

AI in Cybersecurity

Preface

Introduction to AI in Cybersecurity

In an era where technology evolves at an unprecedented pace, cybersecurity has emerged as one of the most critical challenges for organizations, governments, and individuals alike. The rise of sophisticated cyber threats demands equally advanced solutions, and Artificial Intelligence (AI) has emerged as a game-changing force in this domain. AI in cybersecurity represents the fusion of machine intelligence with security strategies, enabling proactive detection, mitigation, and prevention of threats.

The integration of AI in cybersecurity encompasses a wide range of technologies, including machine learning algorithms, neural networks, natural language processing, and predictive analytics. These tools allow organizations to identify anomalies, predict potential breaches, and respond to threats faster than ever before. This book explores the transformative potential of AI in addressing the complexities of modern cybersecurity challenges, shedding light on its benefits, limitations, and future possibilities.

From understanding the fundamentals of AI to exploring its applications in threat detection, automation, and predictive analytics, this book delves into how AI reshapes the cybersecurity landscape. By incorporating real-world examples, use cases, and insights, it offers a comprehensive view of AI's current state and future in cybersecurity. Through this exploration, readers will gain a deeper appreciation of how AI is a tool and a strategic asset in the fight against cyber threats.

Purpose and Scope of the Book

This book aims to provide an in-depth understanding of how AI technologies intersect with cybersecurity to enhance protection, efficiency, and resilience. In a world where digital transformations are accelerating, the need for innovative and robust security solutions has never been more crucial. This book aims to bridge the gap between theory and practice, offering a holistic view of AI in cybersecurity that is both accessible and actionable.

Key objectives of this book include:

- Explaining foundational concepts of AI and cybersecurity, ensuring readers understand the basics before delving into advanced topics.

- Exploring the history and evolution of AI in cyber defense, providing context for its current applications and potential future advancements.

- Presenting practical use cases and tools that leverage AI to combat threats, with a focus on real-world scenarios that demonstrate the effectiveness of AI-driven solutions.

- Discussing the ethical implications and potential risks of AI in cybersecurity, including concerns about bias, privacy, and misuse.

- Offering actionable insights and best practices for implementing AI-driven solutions, ensuring readers can apply the knowledge gained to their own contexts.

- Highlighting career opportunities and the future trajectory of AI in cybersecurity, equipping readers with the information needed to navigate this dynamic field.

The scope of this book extends beyond technical details to include strategic, operational, and ethical considerations, ensuring a well-rounded perspective. It addresses the needs of diverse stakeholders, from technical experts to business leaders, providing a resource that is as versatile as it is informative.

Who Should Read This Book?

This book is tailored for a diverse audience, including:

- **Cybersecurity Professionals**: Gain insights into AI-driven tools and strategies to enhance security operations, streamline workflows, and mitigate risks effectively.

- **IT Managers and Executives**: Understand how AI can be integrated into organizational security frameworks to strengthen defenses and align with business goals.

- **Data Scientists and AI Enthusiasts**: Explore how AI models are applied to solve cybersecurity challenges, with detailed discussions on algorithms, data preparation, and deployment.

- **Students and Academics**: Build foundational knowledge in AI and cybersecurity, supplemented with real-world examples and case studies that bridge the gap between theory and practice.

- **Business Leaders and Decision Makers**: Learn the benefits of AI in mitigating cyber risks, improving business resilience, and driving innovation.

- **Anyone Interested in Technology**: Discover the transformative impact of AI on one of the most pressing global issues of our time, regardless of technical background.

Whether you are a seasoned expert looking to deepen your understanding or a curious learner exploring the field for the first time, this book provides valuable knowledge to help you navigate the intersection of AI and cybersecurity. The content is structured to cater to varying levels of expertise, ensuring every reader finds something valuable.

Chapter 1: Introduction to Artificial Intelligence and Cybersecurity

Introduction

Artificial Intelligence (AI) and cybersecurity are two transformative forces shaping the digital era. With its ability to process vast datasets, identify patterns, and automate decision-making, AI offers unprecedented potential for enhancing cybersecurity measures. At the same time, the evolving threat landscape demands innovative solutions to counter increasingly sophisticated adversaries. This chapter sets the stage for understanding how AI and cybersecurity intersect, exploring their definitions, historical context, challenges, and the global dynamics of cyber threats.

The rapid integration of AI into cybersecurity practices marks a pivotal shift in the battle against cybercrime. From predictive threat analysis to automated incident response, AI-driven solutions are redefining how organizations protect their digital assets. However, the dual-edged nature of AI—serving both defenders and attackers—underscores the need for a nuanced understanding of its role in this field.

1.1 What is Artificial Intelligence?

Artificial Intelligence (AI) refers to the simulation of human intelligence in machines designed to think, reason, and learn. It encompasses various technologies, including machine learning, natural language processing, computer vision, and robotics. These systems can process vast amounts of data, identify patterns, and make decisions, often surpassing human capabilities in speed and accuracy.

AI can be broadly classified into three types:

- **Narrow AI**: Specialized systems designed to perform a specific task, such as image recognition or spam filtering.

- **General AI**: Systems that exhibit human-like intelligence and can perform a wide variety of tasks. While still theoretical, this is the ultimate goal of AI research.

- **Super AI**: Hypothetical AI that surpasses human intelligence across all fields. This remains a speculative concept for now.

AI's applications span industries, from healthcare and finance to transportation and, importantly, cybersecurity, where it plays a pivotal role in automating and enhancing defensive measures.

1.2 The Intersection of AI and Cybersecurity

The convergence of AI and cybersecurity represents a transformative shift in how organizations address and mitigate cyber threats. AI's ability to process large datasets and adapt to emerging patterns aligns perfectly with the dynamic nature of cybersecurity challenges.

Key Contributions of AI in Cybersecurity:

- **Threat Detection**: AI-powered systems analyze vast amounts of network traffic data to identify anomalies that indicate potential attacks.

- **Incident Response**: Automation enables faster reaction to security breaches, minimizing damage and downtime.

- **Predictive Analysis**: Machine learning algorithms anticipate threats before they materialize, enabling proactive defenses.

- **Fraud Detection**: AI models monitor and flag suspicious transactions or behaviors in real-time.

This intersection enhances the efficiency of cybersecurity operations and ensures scalability in addressing the growing complexity of digital threats.

1.3 The Evolution of Cybersecurity Threats

Cybersecurity threats have evolved significantly over the decades, paralleling advancements in technology. Understanding this evolution provides context for AI's critical role in defending against these threats.

Key Milestones in Cybersecurity Threat Evolution:

- **1980s**: The emergence of computer viruses, such as the Brain virus, marked the beginning of malicious software.

- **1990s**: The rise of email-based threats like phishing and the proliferation of malware.

- **2000s**: Advanced persistent threats (APTs) targeting critical infrastructure and large-scale data breaches.

- **2010s**: State-sponsored cyberattacks, ransomware, and sophisticated social engineering tactics.

- **2020s**: The surge in AI-driven attacks and the exploitation of vulnerabilities in IoT devices and cloud platforms.

These developments underscore the need for AI to counter increasingly advanced and persistent adversaries.

1.4 The Role of AI in Modern Cyber Defense

AI has become a cornerstone of modern cyber defense strategies, offering capabilities that traditional security measures cannot match. Its role spans multiple dimensions of cybersecurity:

- **Real-Time Threat Monitoring**: AI systems analyze network activity in real-time to detect and respond to threats instantaneously.

- **Behavioral Analytics**: Machine learning models profile user behavior to identify unusual activities indicative of breaches.

- **Enhanced Security Operations Centers (SOCs)**: AI tools assist SOCs by prioritizing alerts, reducing false positives, and automating routine tasks.

- **Endpoint Protection**: AI enhances endpoint security by identifying and blocking malicious activities on devices.

- **Adaptive Learning**: AI systems continuously learn and evolve to counter new attack vectors and tactics.

These advancements demonstrate how AI empowers organizations to maintain robust defenses in an ever-changing threat landscape.

1.5 Challenges in Cybersecurity Today

Despite technological progress, cybersecurity remains fraught with challenges. Understanding these challenges highlights the areas where AI can impact most.

Major Challenges:

- **Volume of Threats**: The sheer number of cyber threats makes it difficult for human analysts to keep pace.

- **Sophistication of Attacks**: Adversaries use advanced techniques, including AI, to bypass traditional defenses.

- **Skill Shortages**: A global shortage of cybersecurity professionals leaves organizations vulnerable.

- **Privacy Concerns**: Balancing data collection for security purposes with user privacy remains a persistent issue.

- **Regulatory Compliance**: Adhering to complex and evolving regulations adds another layer of difficulty for organizations.

These challenges underline the urgency of adopting AI-driven solutions to bolster defenses and address systemic vulnerabilities.

1.6 The Global Landscape of Cyber Threats

Cyber threats are no longer confined to individual actors; they now encompass a global network of adversaries, ranging from hackers to nation-states. This section provides an overview of the diverse threat actors and their motivations:

Types of Threat Actors:

- **Hacktivists**: Ideologically motivated individuals or groups targeting entities for political or social reasons.

- **Cybercriminals**: Profit-driven attackers engaging in activities like ransomware, phishing, and fraud.

- **Nation-State Actors**: Governments conducting cyber espionage, sabotage, and warfare to advance geopolitical interests.

- **Insiders**: Employees or contractors who misuse their access to compromise systems, often for personal or financial gain.

Emerging Trends:

- **AI-Powered Attacks**: Adversaries leveraging AI for automated phishing, deepfake-based scams, and advanced malware.

- **Supply Chain Attacks**: Exploiting vulnerabilities in third-party vendors to infiltrate larger networks.

- **Critical Infrastructure Targeting**: Threats against essential energy, healthcare, and transportation services.

Understanding the global threat landscape is essential for crafting AI-driven solutions that address both current and emerging challenges.

Summary

The integration of Artificial Intelligence into cybersecurity represents a groundbreaking advancement in combating cyber threats. This chapter has explored the foundational aspects of AI, its convergence with cybersecurity, and the evolving threat landscape. This chapter sets the stage for understanding AI's transformative role in modern cyber defense by delving into the history, contributions, challenges, and global dynamics. As we progress through this book, the focus will shift to the practical applications, tools, and best practices that enable organizations to leverage AI effectively in their cybersecurity strategies. Together, these insights will empower readers to confidently navigate the complex and ever-changing digital security environment.

Chapter 2: The History of AI in Cybersecurity

Introduction

The journey of Artificial Intelligence (AI) in cybersecurity is marked by continuous evolution as advancements in AI align with the increasing complexity of digital threats. From its early conceptualization to its integration into modern cyber defense systems, AI has significantly influenced how organizations identify, mitigate, and prevent cyberattacks. This chapter delves into the historical milestones, pivotal innovations, and transformative impact of AI in cybersecurity, providing a comprehensive understanding of its past, present, and future.

2.1 Early Concepts and Theories of AI

The origins of Artificial Intelligence (AI) can be traced back to the mid-20th century when visionaries and pioneers began exploring the possibility of machines replicating human intelligence. Key figures like Alan Turing and John McCarthy were instrumental in shaping AI as a formal field of study.

The Pioneering Foundations

- **Alan Turing's Influence**: In his groundbreaking paper, "Computing Machinery and Intelligence" (1950), Alan Turing proposed the concept of machines capable of performing tasks that would typically require human intelligence. He introduced the Turing Test, a method to evaluate a machine's ability to exhibit intelligent behavior indistinguishable from that of a human. This idea laid the groundwork for defining intelligence in computational systems.

- **John McCarthy and the Term "Artificial Intelligence"**: In 1956, John McCarthy organized the Dartmouth Conference, marking the formal birth of AI as a discipline. McCarthy's definition of AI emphasized creating machines that could perform tasks requiring human-like reasoning, problem-solving, and learning.

Key Early Theories and Paradigms

- **Symbolic AI**: Symbolic AI, also known as "Good Old-Fashioned AI" (GOFAI), focuses on using symbols and predefined rules to represent knowledge and solve problems. The approach relied on logical reasoning, making it suitable for structured problems such as chess or theorem proving. While symbolic AI provided initial successes, it struggled with unstructured data and real-world complexities.

- **Machine Learning**: Early machine learning methods emerged as an alternative to symbolic AI. Instead of relying on explicit rules, these systems learned patterns from data to make predictions and decisions. This approach paved the way for modern algorithms that improve their performance over time, adapting to changing environments—a critical capability in cybersecurity applications.

- **Neural Networks**: Inspired by the structure and functioning of the human brain, neural networks were conceptualized to enable machines to recognize patterns and make decisions. Initial efforts, such as Frank Rosenblatt's perceptron (1958), laid the foundation for today's deep learning systems. These networks became instrumental in tasks like image recognition, natural language processing, and anomaly detection in cybersecurity.

<u>Relevance to Cybersecurity</u>

Though conceptualized decades ago, the foundational theories of AI directly influence modern cybersecurity practices. For instance:

- **Symbolic AI**: Its rule-based systems are used in access control mechanisms and expert systems for threat analysis.

- **Machine Learning**: Drives intrusion detection systems (IDS) and predictive analytics for identifying potential vulnerabilities.

- **Neural Networks**: Enhance real-time threat detection by analyzing network traffic and identifying anomalies indicative of attacks.

These early developments shaped AI as a discipline and set the stage for its integration into cybersecurity, addressing challenges posed by increasingly sophisticated cyber threats.

2.2 The Development of Cybersecurity Measures

The field of cybersecurity has evolved in tandem with technological advancements, with each era bringing forth new defensive measures to counter emerging threats. From the early days of rudimentary protections to today's sophisticated systems, the development of cybersecurity has been marked by innovation and adaptation.

<u>Milestones in Cybersecurity Development</u>

1. **1970s: The Dawn of Antivirus Software**
   - The emergence of early computer viruses, such as the Creeper virus, prompted the creation of the first antivirus software. These tools aimed to detect, quarantine, and remove malicious programs from infected systems.
   - Researchers like Ray Tomlinson developed programs like Reaper to combat early threats, marking the genesis of defensive cybersecurity tools.
2. **1980s: Firewalls and Network Security**

- The rise of personal computers and interconnected networks led to the invention of firewalls designed to filter incoming and outgoing network traffic. These systems provided a barrier against unauthorized access.
- Packet-filtering firewalls and, later, stateful inspection firewalls became essential in securing enterprise networks.

3. **1990s: Encryption and Intrusion Detection Systems**
   - With the proliferation of the internet, securing data in transit became crucial. Encryption protocols like SSL (Secure Sockets Layer) were introduced to protect online communications.
   - Intrusion Detection Systems (IDS) emerged as a critical technology to monitor network traffic for suspicious activity, providing alerts for potential breaches.

4. **2000s: Multifactor Authentication and Endpoint Protection**
   - The early 2000s saw the widespread adoption of multifactor authentication (MFA), enhancing security by requiring multiple forms of verification.
   - Advanced endpoint protection solutions emerged to safeguard individual devices against malware, ransomware, and zero-day attacks.

5. **2010s: Cloud-Based Security and Threat Intelligence**
   - The shift to cloud computing brought about cloud-based security solutions, enabling scalable and centralized protection for organizations.
   - Platforms for sharing threat intelligence among organizations became common, fostering collaboration to combat global cyber threats.

6. **2020s: AI-Driven Cybersecurity**
   - The integration of AI in cybersecurity has revolutionized threat detection and response. AI-driven tools analyze vast amounts of data in real-time, identifying anomalies

and preventing attacks with unprecedented speed and accuracy.

The Impact of Cybersecurity Evolution

Each milestone in cybersecurity development has addressed specific challenges posed by evolving technology and threats. The integration of AI into cybersecurity builds upon this foundation, offering enhanced capabilities to detect, prevent, and respond to complex attacks. From the early days of basic antivirus programs to today's AI-driven threat intelligence platforms, the journey of cybersecurity reflects continuous innovation aimed at protecting the digital ecosystem.

2.3 AI's Early Applications in Cybersecurity

Artificial Intelligence (AI) 's initial applications in cybersecurity centered on enhancing efficiency, automating repetitive tasks, and improving the detection of anomalies in network traffic. These foundational use cases paved the way for today's sophisticated AI-driven solutions.

Early Use Cases of AI in Cybersecurity

1. **Spam Filters**:
   o One of the first practical applications of AI in cybersecurity was the development of spam filters. Machine learning models were trained to identify and filter spam emails based on patterns, keywords, and sender behavior.
   o By analyzing large datasets of email communications, these filters learned to differentiate between legitimate and malicious messages, reducing phishing attempts and other email-based threats.
2. **Anomaly Detection**:
   o AI algorithms were deployed to monitor network traffic and identify unusual patterns or behaviors indicative of potential threats.

- o Early anomaly detection systems relied on statistical models and basic machine learning techniques to flag deviations from normal activity, such as unusual login locations or abnormal data transfer volumes.

3. **Log Analysis**:
   - o The manual review of system logs was a time-consuming and error-prone task. AI introduced automation to this process by analyzing logs for irregularities, prioritizing alerts, and highlighting potential security incidents.
   - o This application significantly reduced response times, enabling security teams to focus on critical threats.

Limitations of Early AI Applications

While these early AI-driven solutions marked a significant advancement in cybersecurity, they also faced several challenges:

- **Limited Data Availability**: Early systems often lacked the vast datasets needed for robust machine learning models.
- **High False Positive Rates**: Initial algorithms frequently generated false alarms, requiring human intervention to validate threats.
- **Computational Constraints**: The computational power required for training and deploying AI models was limited, restricting their scalability and effectiveness.

Legacy and Influence on Modern Systems

Despite their limitations, these early applications demonstrated the potential of AI to transform cybersecurity. They:

- Established the importance of automation in managing large-scale cyber threats.

- Highlighted the need for continuous improvement and adaptation of AI models to evolving threat landscapes.

- Laid the groundwork for advanced systems such as behavioral analytics, predictive threat modeling, and AI-driven security orchestration.

These early innovations are the foundation for cutting-edge AI technologies that protect critical infrastructure, sensitive data, and digital assets worldwide.

2.4 Milestones and Innovations in AI for Cyber Defense

Artificial Intelligence (AI) has been a transformative force in cybersecurity, continuously evolving to counteract increasingly sophisticated cyber threats. Each milestone in the integration of AI into cyber defense marks a leap forward in protecting digital assets.

Early AI Milestones in Cyber Defense

1. **2000s: Supervised and Unsupervised Learning for Malware Detection**
   o **Supervised Learning**: AI systems trained on labeled datasets began identifying known malware patterns with remarkable accuracy. This approach helped antivirus solutions transition from signature-based detection to more dynamic models capable of identifying previously unseen threats.
   o **Unsupervised Learning**: By clustering and identifying anomalies in data without predefined labels, AI systems started recognizing zero-day malware, which operates without known signatures.
2. **2010s: Behavioral Analytics and Insider Threat Detection**
   o Behavioral analytics revolutionized the detection of insider threats by creating individual profiles for users and monitoring deviations from their typical behavior.
   o For example, unusual file access patterns or logins from atypical locations triggered automated alerts, reducing the time required to identify internal risks.

3. **Mid-2010s: Natural Language Processing (NLP) for Phishing Detection**
   - o NLP models were deployed to analyze the content of emails, identifying phishing attempts by examining tone, structure, and suspicious URLs.
   - o This innovation significantly reduced the success rate of email-based social engineering attacks, particularly spear phishing campaigns targeting high-value individuals.
4. **Late 2010s: AI-Driven Threat Intelligence Platforms**
   - o AI-enabled platforms aggregated threat data from global sources, identifying patterns and emerging attack vectors.
   - o These platforms empowered organizations to implement proactive defenses by leveraging predictive analytics to anticipate and counteract potential threats.

Recent Innovations Transforming Cyber Defense

1. **2020s: Generative AI in Deception-Based Strategies**
   - o Generative AI, such as GANs (Generative Adversarial Networks), is now used to create highly realistic decoys or "honeypots."
   - o These decoys lure attackers into interacting with fake systems, diverting their efforts and revealing their tactics, tools, and procedures (TTPs).
2. **AI for Advanced Persistent Threat (APT) Detection**
   - o AI models analyze vast volumes of data to uncover APTs that remain undetected for extended periods.
   - o By correlating data across endpoints, networks, and cloud environments, AI identifies subtle indicators of compromise (IoCs), reducing attacker dwell time.
3. **Real-Time Automated Incident Response**
   - o AI-powered security orchestration and automation platforms (SOAR) now enable real-time response to incidents.

- o These systems autonomously quarantine affected devices, block malicious IPs, and generate comprehensive reports, minimizing damage and improving efficiency.

4. **Adversarial AI and Countermeasures**
   - o As cybercriminals leverage AI to bypass defenses, cybersecurity systems have adapted to counter adversarial AI tactics.
   - o These countermeasures include enhancing model robustness, detecting poisoned datasets, and deploying adaptive learning algorithms to maintain an edge over attackers.

Benefits of AI in Cyber Defense

- **Scalability**: AI systems process massive datasets across global infrastructures, making them invaluable for enterprises managing vast networks.
- **Speed**: Real-time detection and response ensure minimal damage and disruption.
- **Accuracy**: Advanced models improve precision, reducing false positives and negatives compared to earlier systems.
- **Proactivity**: Predictive analytics allow organizations to identify and mitigate threats before they materialize.

AI's Evolving Role in the Cybersecurity Landscape

The milestones and innovations in AI-driven cyber defense showcase its journey from basic anomaly detection to sophisticated, autonomous systems capable of addressing modern cyber threats. As AI continues to evolve, its integration into cybersecurity will expand further, ensuring it remains a critical asset in defending against an increasingly complex threat landscape.

2.5 AI and the Emergence of Modern Cyber Threats

The rapid advancement of AI has ushered in a new era of cyber threats, dramatically changing the landscape of cybersecurity. As artificial intelligence becomes more sophisticated, so too do the methods employed by cyber adversaries. Attackers have quickly adopted AI and machine learning techniques to enhance their offensive capabilities, enabling them to create more targeted, adaptive, and evasive threats. The dual-use nature of AI — its potential to be used for both beneficial and malicious purposes — underscores the pressing need for robust, evolving defenses to protect against the misuse of this powerful technology by cybercriminals.

Examples of AI-Driven Threats:

1. **Automated Phishing Campaigns:** One of the most common and concerning ways AI is being leveraged in cyberattacks is through automated phishing campaigns. AI systems can be used to craft highly personalized and convincing phishing emails, making it easier for attackers to deceive individuals or organizations into revealing sensitive information. AI-driven tools can analyze social media profiles, news articles, and other data sources to tailor these emails to the target's interests, relationships, or even recent activities. This makes the phishing attempts far more convincing, increasing the likelihood of a successful attack.

   For example, an AI algorithm could analyze an executive's calendar and emails to create a phishing email that mimics a trusted colleague or business partner request. By automating the creation of these emails, attackers can launch large-scale campaigns that are harder to detect and block, as they appear highly legitimate.

2. **Deepfake Attacks:** Deepfakes, powered by generative AI techniques, have emerged as a powerful weapon in the hands of

cybercriminals. These AI-generated synthetic media — including videos, images, and audio — are created by training machine learning models on existing media to generate hyper-realistic but entirely fabricated content.

Cybercriminals can use deepfakes for a variety of malicious purposes, such as impersonating key figures in an organization or government to manipulate or deceive others. For example, attackers may create a deepfake video of a CEO appearing to make an announcement about a financial transaction, fooling employees or stakeholders into transferring funds to the attacker's accounts. Similarly, deepfake audio could be used to convincingly impersonate a voice, leading to fraudulent wire transfers or confidential information being disclosed over the phone.

3. **Adversarial AI:** Adversarial AI refers to the manipulation of AI systems by introducing deceptive or misleading data to bypass detection mechanisms or cause incorrect outputs. This type of attack targets the vulnerabilities in machine learning models, which are often designed to detect and mitigate threats based on patterns of behavior or data analysis. By feeding adversarial examples into an AI system, attackers can trick the system into making incorrect predictions, classifications, or decisions.

   For example, adversarial AI could be used to manipulate a cybersecurity system's intrusion detection algorithm, causing it to misclassify a cyberattack as legitimate network traffic. Similarly, adversaries could use adversarial machine learning to bypass facial recognition systems or content moderation filters, leading to unauthorized access or the spread of harmful content.

The Dual-Use Nature of AI:

While AI holds immense potential to enhance cybersecurity, it also provides malicious actors with powerful tools to exploit vulnerabilities and bypass defenses. The dual-use nature of AI — its ability to be used for both defensive and offensive purposes — highlights the critical need for continuous innovation in cybersecurity strategies. As AI evolves, so too must the mechanisms designed to protect against its misuse.

To defend against AI-driven threats, organizations must develop advanced AI-powered security solutions that recognize and mitigate malicious AI techniques. Additionally, a proactive approach to cybersecurity is essential, focusing on threat detection, rapid response, and real-time monitoring to combat the growing sophistication of AI-driven attacks. Cybersecurity professionals must also prioritize AI ethics, ensuring that AI technologies are developed and deployed responsibly to prevent them from being weaponized by bad actors.

2.6 How AI Has Transformed the Cybersecurity Industry

The integration of AI into cybersecurity has ushered in profound changes, reshaping how organizations detect, respond to, and prevent cyber threats. As the sophistication of cyberattacks continues to evolve, AI has become an indispensable tool, providing new ways to enhance security measures and streamline the defense process. By enabling faster, more accurate, and proactive responses, AI is strengthening existing security frameworks and creating new approaches to safeguarding sensitive data, systems, and networks.

Transformative Impacts:

1. **Real-Time Analysis:** AI-powered tools have significantly improved the speed at which threats are detected and analyzed. Traditionally, cybersecurity systems relied on predefined signatures or rule-based systems to identify threats, which could

result in slow detection times and missed threats. However, with AI and machine learning (ML), security systems can now process and analyze vast amounts of data in real-time, identifying potential threats as they arise.

This ability to analyze large datasets instantaneously allows organizations to respond to attacks in near real-time. AI-powered systems can detect patterns, anomalies, and behaviors that may indicate malicious activity, giving cybersecurity teams valuable insights into evolving threats and enabling them to take immediate action. This reduction in response times is crucial for mitigating damage and protecting critical infrastructure from cyberattacks.

2. **Scalability:** One of the most significant challenges in cybersecurity is managing the sheer volume of data generated by modern networks and systems. The complexity of cyber threats continues to grow as attackers employ more sophisticated methods and technologies. AI has revolutionized the way organizations scale their cybersecurity defenses to keep up with this growing complexity.

   AI and machine learning allow for automated data analysis, which means security systems can process and interpret massive datasets without overwhelming human analysts. This scalability enables organizations to manage increasingly complex infrastructures and environments, including cloud-based systems, IoT devices, and remote work environments, without compromising security. AI tools can adapt and evolve as new threats emerge, ensuring that cybersecurity defenses remain robust as the attack surface expands.

3. **Reduced False Positives:** One of the common issues in traditional cybersecurity systems is the generation of false positives — benign activities that are incorrectly flagged as

threats. These false alarms create "alert fatigue" for security teams, leading to missed real threats, decreased efficiency, and burnout among cybersecurity professionals. AI-driven systems have made great strides in addressing this problem by improving threat detection accuracy.

Through machine learning and continuous training, AI systems can better distinguish between legitimate and malicious activities, reducing the number of false positives. By analyzing vast datasets and learning from past incidents, AI systems can detect subtle, sophisticated threats that traditional methods may overlook. This reduction in false positives enhances the accuracy of threat detection and allows cybersecurity teams to focus their resources on responding to real threats rather than wasting time on irrelevant alerts.

4. **Proactive Defense:** One of the most powerful capabilities of AI in cybersecurity is its ability to predict and prevent attacks before they occur. AI-powered systems leverage predictive analytics, utilizing historical data, threat intelligence, and machine learning models to identify patterns and trends that could indicate an imminent attack. By proactively identifying vulnerabilities and risks, AI can help organizations stay one step ahead of cybercriminals.

Predictive defense capabilities enable security teams to prioritize resources and fortify the most vulnerable areas of their network before an attack happens. For example, AI can detect early indicators of a zero-day exploit or a phishing campaign, allowing organizations to take preventive measures, such as patching vulnerabilities, enhancing network defenses, or launching threat-hunting activities. This proactive approach shifts cybersecurity from a reactive model, where responses are made after the fact, to a more anticipatory and preventative stance, which is crucial in today's fast-evolving threat landscape.

<u>The Pivotal Role of AI in Modernizing Cybersecurity Operations:</u>

The transformation brought about by AI in cybersecurity goes beyond just technological advancements; it fundamentally changes how organizations approach security at every level. AI has moved the industry from traditional, signature-based detection methods to dynamic, adaptive, and predictive models that continuously learn from new data and threats. This shift is essential in an era where cyber threats are more sophisticated, targeted, and frequent than ever before.

As AI continues to evolve, its role in cybersecurity will only grow more significant. From automating routine tasks to providing real-time insights and proactive defense, AI is revolutionizing the way cybersecurity teams operate. By enhancing the accuracy, scalability, and speed of threat detection and response, AI strengthens security defenses and helps organizations better manage their resources, reduce costs, and minimize the risks associated with cyberattacks.

2.7 AI and Its Role in the Future of Cybersecurity

The future of cybersecurity is increasingly tied to the advancements in artificial intelligence (AI), as emerging technologies are set to redefine how organizations approach digital threats. AI's growing sophistication promises to play a pivotal role in shaping the landscape of cybersecurity in the coming years, enhancing existing defenses and enabling entirely new strategies for protecting data, systems, and networks. As AI continues to evolve, several key trends and technologies are poised to transform the way cybersecurity is practiced, offering more robust, proactive, and adaptive defense mechanisms.

<u>Emerging Trends:</u>

1. **Explainable AI (XAI):** One of the major challenges of AI in cybersecurity (and other fields) is its "black-box" nature, where AI models make decisions or predictions without providing a

clear explanation for how they arrived at those conclusions. This lack of transparency can hinder trust in AI systems, particularly in critical sectors such as cybersecurity, where decisions made by AI can have significant consequences. To address this issue, **Explainable AI (XAI)** is emerging as a solution that ensures transparency and accountability in AI-driven decisions.

XAI provides a framework where AI models can make decisions and explain how those decisions were made in human-understandable terms. This is crucial in cybersecurity, as it allows analysts to understand the reasoning behind an AI system's threat detection or response, helping them trust and refine AI-assisted decision-making processes. XAI will ensure that cybersecurity teams can rely on AI technologies and intervene when necessary to improve outcomes. Furthermore, it fosters accountability and compliance with regulatory requirements in industries where transparency is critical.

2. **Quantum Computing: Quantum computing** represents a revolutionary leap in computational power, harnessing the principles of quantum mechanics to perform tasks that would be impossible or prohibitively slow for classical computers. While quantum computing promises to unlock significant advances in fields such as drug discovery and material science, it also poses a major threat to traditional encryption methods. Quantum computers could break existing cryptographic algorithms, foundational to cybersecurity today.

To address this challenge, AI is expected to play a pivotal role in developing new cryptographic solutions that are resistant to quantum-powered attacks. **AI-enhanced cryptography**, such as post-quantum cryptographic algorithms, will be designed to withstand the capabilities of quantum computers while ensuring the integrity and confidentiality of sensitive data. AI will also be used to monitor and adapt cryptographic systems in real-time, providing dynamic responses to emerging quantum threats. As quantum computing evolves, the integration of AI into cybersecurity solutions will be essential for building resilient and future-proof security infrastructures.

3. **Autonomous Defense Systems:** The rise of **autonomous defense systems** will mark a significant evolution in the way organizations protect their digital assets. These systems leverage AI to create **self-healing networks** capable of independently identifying and mitigating threats without human intervention. Autonomous defense systems will use machine learning algorithms to continuously monitor network traffic, detect anomalous behavior, and adapt to new types of attacks as they emerge.

   Self-healing networks could autonomously isolate compromised systems, reconfigure firewalls, or apply patches to vulnerabilities in real-time. By automating the detection and response to threats, these systems can significantly reduce the time it takes to mitigate an attack, minimizing the damage caused by cybercriminals. Additionally, autonomous defense systems will enable organizations to focus on more strategic tasks, while the AI-driven systems handle the routine aspects of cybersecurity. The increased autonomy will allow security teams to address complex challenges and focus on higher-level decision-making, ultimately leading to faster, more efficient defense strategies.

Anticipated Benefits:

1. **Enhanced Collaboration Between AI Systems and Human Analysts:** As AI continues to evolve, it will not replace human analysts but empower them to make more informed decisions and act more effectively. The collaboration between AI and human experts will create a symbiotic relationship where AI augments the capabilities of cybersecurity professionals, allowing

them to identify threats more quickly and accurately. Human analysts will still play a critical role in interpreting AI-driven insights, managing complex incidents, and providing context-sensitive judgment in scenarios where AI may struggle.

AI's ability to process large amounts of data, detect patterns, and analyze evolving threats in real-time will give analysts the tools they need to respond more swiftly and effectively. Combining AI's computational power, human intuition, and experience will foster a more dynamic, adaptable, and proactive cybersecurity environment.

2. **Greater Accessibility to AI-Driven Tools for Small and Medium-Sized Enterprises (SMEs):** Historically, AI-powered advanced cybersecurity tools were predominantly available to large enterprises with significant resources. However, the growing accessibility of AI technology means that small and medium-sized enterprises (SMEs) can also leverage AI-driven cybersecurity solutions. This democratization of AI technology will allow SMEs to protect themselves from cyber threats that they may have previously been unable to defend against due to cost or complexity.

    AI-powered cybersecurity tools, such as automated threat detection, real-time response, and predictive analytics, will enable SMEs to implement robust security measures without the need for large, dedicated cybersecurity teams. This shift will reduce the cybersecurity divide between small businesses and larger corporations, ensuring that organizations of all sizes can benefit from the enhanced protection offered by AI-driven tools.

3. **Improved Integration of AI with Other Technologies, Such as Blockchain and IoT Security:** As the cybersecurity landscape becomes increasingly interconnected, the integration of AI with other emerging technologies will be crucial for

providing comprehensive protection. **Blockchain**, for instance, offers the potential for secure, decentralized systems that could complement AI's capabilities in areas like data integrity and authentication. AI can be used to enhance blockchain security by detecting fraudulent activities, ensuring the integrity of decentralized transactions, and automating blockchain governance.

The integration of AI with **Internet of Things (IoT) security** will also play a key role in securing the ever-growing number of connected devices. AI can be used to monitor IoT networks in real-time, identifying vulnerabilities, preventing attacks, and ensuring that IoT devices operate securely. This collaboration between AI, blockchain, and IoT security technologies will create a more holistic, multi-layered approach to cybersecurity, addressing the diverse and evolving threats the digital ecosystem poses.

Summary

The history of AI in cybersecurity reflects a journey of innovation and adaptation, with each phase building upon the last to address increasingly complex challenges. From its early theoretical foundations to its transformative impact on the cybersecurity industry, AI has proven to be a game-changer in the fight against cyber threats. As we look to the future, the continued evolution of AI promises to empower organizations with smarter, more effective defenses while addressing the dual-use concerns of this powerful technology. This chapter has provided a comprehensive overview of AI's historical and ongoing contributions to cybersecurity, setting the stage for deeper exploration in the subsequent chapters.

Chapter 3: Understanding Generative AI

Introduction

Generative AI represents one of the most revolutionary advancements in artificial intelligence, offering capabilities that extend far beyond traditional AI systems. The technology's ability to create new, realistic content across various domains has implications that extend to cybersecurity. This chapter dives deep into the various aspects of Generative AI, focusing on its models, applications, ethical challenges, risks, and future in the context of cybersecurity.

3.1 Defining Generative AI

Generative AI refers to a subset of artificial intelligence techniques designed to produce new, original content based on learned patterns from data. Unlike traditional AI, typically used for classification, recognition, or prediction tasks, generative AI goes a step further by enabling machines to generate entirely new data—text, images, audio, or even video—based on input data.

At the core of Generative AI are machine learning algorithms that are trained on large datasets to understand the underlying structures of the data. This allows them to mimic or produce variations of the input data. The primary types of models that power generative AI include:

- **Generative Adversarial Networks (GANs):** GANs use two neural networks, the generator and the discriminator, working in opposition to each other. The generator creates new data, and the discriminator evaluates its authenticity. Through continuous feedback from the discriminator, the generator improves its ability to create realistic data, such as images or sounds.

- **Variational Autoencoders (VAEs):** VAEs compress input data into a latent space and then reconstruct it. The model learns to generate new, similar data that approximates the original data distribution. VAEs are often used for applications that require the generation of smooth and continuous outputs.

- **Transformer Models:** Transformer-based models, such as **GPT (Generative Pre-trained Transformer)** and **BERT**, are primarily used in natural language processing (NLP). These models can generate highly coherent and contextually relevant text. Their ability to understand and produce human-like text has revolutionized content creation, chatbots, and even automated code generation.

Generative AI has significant implications for various industries, including cybersecurity, where its potential can both strengthen defenses and be exploited for malicious purposes.

3.2 Generative AI Models and Their Significance

The significance of generative AI models lies in their ability to process data and create new and realistic data based on what they have learned. Below, we delve deeper into the most prominent models and their importance in various fields, including cybersecurity.

- **Generative Adversarial Networks (GANs):** GANs have shown tremendous potential in fields such as image generation, video creation, and synthetic data production. Their ability to create realistic images, sounds, and videos has entertainment, art, and security implications. In cybersecurity, GANs can be used for attack simulations and vulnerability testing, generating malware variants, or simulating phishing attempts to test defense mechanisms.

- **Variational Autoencoders (VAEs):** VAEs are significant

because they allow the generation of highly structured data that adheres to the characteristics of the original dataset. These models are useful in fields like healthcare and finance for generating synthetic data that maintains the statistical properties of sensitive information without exposing actual data, helping organizations comply with privacy regulations. In cybersecurity, VAEs can generate realistic attack scenarios for testing security systems, ensuring that defenses can handle new and previously unseen threats.

- **Transformer Models (e.g., GPT, BERT):** These models have revolutionized NLP, enabling machines to generate human-like text that can be used for various applications such as content creation, automated customer support, and more. In cybersecurity, these models can be leveraged to generate phishing emails, social engineering scripts, or fake social media profiles for simulating attacks. Their capacity to generate coherent and contextually relevant content makes them potent tools for both offense and defense.

The significance of these models cannot be overstated. They expand the potential for innovation in cybersecurity, from improving threat detection and response to helping organizations anticipate and prevent future attacks.

3.3 How Generative AI Is Applied in Cybersecurity

Generative AI is not just a theoretical concept in cybersecurity—it is being actively applied in numerous areas to enhance defenses, predict attacks, and train AI models. Below are several notable applications:

- **Threat Simulation and Penetration Testing:** Generative AI can be used to simulate sophisticated attacks, such as advanced persistent threats (APTs) and zero-day exploits. By generating AI-driven malware, penetration testers can assess the resilience of an organization's security infrastructure against highly plausible attack scenarios. This allows organizations to identify weaknesses and strengthen their defenses before real attacks occur.

- **Synthetic Data Generation for AI Training:** One of the biggest challenges in cybersecurity is the lack of labeled data for training machine learning models. Generative AI can create synthetic datasets that mimic real-world attacks or threats without exposing sensitive data. This is especially useful in training AI systems for intrusion detection, anomaly detection, and malware classification tasks.

- **Automated Incident Response:** Generative AI can also play a role in automated incident response. In the event of a detected attack, AI models can generate the appropriate responses, such as blocking malicious IP addresses, isolating infected machines, or adjusting firewall settings. These automatic actions significantly reduce the response time, which is critical during active threats.

- **Behavioral Analysis and Anomaly Detection:** Generative AI can be used to generate normal behavior patterns for users and systems, which can then be used to identify anomalies. For example, by creating a model of what normal network traffic looks like, generative AI can help security systems detect unusual activity that may indicate a potential cyberattack, even if the attack is novel and not previously seen.

3.4 Ethical Considerations of Generative AI in Cybersecurity

While generative AI offers tremendous potential for improving cybersecurity, it also raises several ethical concerns. These concerns stem from the technology's capacity to create highly realistic content that can be used maliciously. Key ethical considerations include:

- **Deepfakes and Misinformation:** Generative AI's ability to create hyper-realistic deepfake videos, audio, and images can be exploited to deceive people or manipulate public perception. Cybercriminals could use deepfakes to impersonate corporate executives, politicians, or celebrities to execute fraud or cause reputational damage. The use of such technology to manipulate truth poses a significant challenge to the integrity of information and trust.

- **Privacy Concerns:** The ability of generative AI to create synthetic data that closely mimics real-world data could lead to privacy violations. For example, if a model is trained on sensitive personal information, it could accidentally generate data that closely resembles real individuals' information, even though the data is synthetic. This could expose organizations to legal risks if the synthetic data is not properly handled.

- **Bias and Discrimination:** Generative AI models are trained on large datasets, and if these datasets are biased, the models will learn and propagate those biases. In cybersecurity, biased AI models could inadvertently create security vulnerabilities for certain user groups or overlook threats that disproportionately affect specific communities. Ensuring fairness and transparency in the training data is essential to avoid reinforcing societal biases.

- **Accountability and Transparency:** The complexity of generative AI models can make it challenging to explain and understand how they arrive at certain decisions. This "black-box" nature of AI is problematic when the AI is used in cybersecurity decision-making processes, where accountability is critical. If an AI system fails to detect an attack or generates a false positive, understanding why the AI made that decision is crucial for both troubleshooting and improving security.

3.5 Case Studies of Generative AI in Cyber Defense

Several real-world case studies demonstrate the practical benefits of generative AI in enhancing cybersecurity efforts. Here are a few examples:

- **AI-Generated Malware for Defensive Training:** A cybersecurity company used a GAN to generate sophisticated, realistic examples of malware. These AI-generated malware samples were used to evaluate and test the detection capabilities of antivirus software and intrusion detection systems (IDS). This helped improve the accuracy and reliability of existing security tools in detecting unknown or advanced malware types.

- **AI-Generated Phishing Emails for Employee Training:** Generative AI models have been used to create convincing phishing emails that mimic real-world attacks. Organizations have used these AI-generated emails in simulated phishing campaigns to educate employees about how to recognize suspicious emails. This proactive approach to employee training helps mitigate the risk of social engineering attacks.

- **Generative AI in Security Automation:** AI-powered systems have been deployed to automatically respond to detected threats. For example, when a ransomware attack was identified, an AI-driven defense system immediately generated a series of countermeasures, such as isolating infected devices, disabling the attacker's communication channels, and restoring backups, thereby limiting the damage and reducing recovery time.

- **AI-Generated Synthetic Attack Scenarios for Threat Intelligence:** A leading cybersecurity firm utilized generative AI to generate synthetic attack scenarios that closely mimicked sophisticated cyberattack tactics, techniques, and procedures (TTPs) used by advanced persistent threats (APTs). These AI-generated attack scenarios were fed into a threat intelligence platform to enhance its ability to detect and mitigate potential threats in real-time. By leveraging this synthetic data, the organization was able to build more accurate threat models, improve early detection systems, and develop better strategies for mitigating zero-day vulnerabilities. This proactive approach allowed the cybersecurity team to anticipate and defend against highly probable attacks that hadn't yet been observed in the wild.

- **AI-Generated Fake Social Media Accounts for Identity Protection:** Generative AI was applied to simulate fake social media profiles, enabling cybersecurity professionals to test social engineering defenses. In this case, AI models created highly convincing fake profiles on various social platforms, such as LinkedIn, Facebook, and Twitter. These profiles were designed to resemble real employees from the target organization and were used to assess the company's susceptibility to spear-phishing, impersonation, and social engineering attacks. By mimicking real employee behaviors and relationships, the AI-generated profiles were able to test how well security measures, such as multi-factor authentication and behavioral analysis, could prevent identity theft and unauthorized access. This case study highlights how generative AI can be used to simulate real-world attacks and fortify identity protection strategies.

3.6 Risks Associated with Generative AI in Cyber Attacks

As much as generative AI enhances cybersecurity, it also opens new avenues for cybercriminals to exploit. Some of the key risks associated with generative AI in cyberattacks include:

- **AI-Generated Malware:** Generative AI could be used to produce malware that adapts over time, making it harder for traditional security tools to detect. By continuously evolving, AI-generated malware could bypass signature-based detection systems and spread rapidly, increasing the scale and speed of cyberattacks.

- **AI-Powered Phishing Attacks:** Generative AI can be used to create highly convincing phishing emails, fake websites, and even voice or video impersonations. These AI-generated phishing attempts are more difficult to detect than traditional phishing, as they can be personalized and crafted to mimic specific individuals, making them appear more legitimate to the target.

- **Automated Vulnerability Exploitation:** Cybercriminals could use generative AI to scan for vulnerabilities and generate exploits autonomously. By automating the discovery and exploitation of weaknesses, attackers could launch widespread attacks with minimal human intervention.

3.7 Addressing the Potential for AI-Driven Malware and Phishing

To mitigate the risks posed by AI-driven cyberattacks, several strategies should be employed:

- **AI-Powered Detection Systems:** Generative AI can be used to enhance cybersecurity defenses by training AI systems to detect novel attack patterns. Machine learning models can be continuously updated with new attack data, allowing them to recognize AI-driven threats and respond accordingly.

- **Human-AI Collaboration:** While AI systems can handle high volumes of data and recognize patterns quickly, human analysts are still necessary to provide context and interpret complex attacks. A collaborative approach, where AI enhances human decision-making, can ensure that cybersecurity efforts are both fast and accurate.

- **Phishing Awareness and User Training:** Organizations should prioritize training their employees to recognize AI-generated phishing emails, fake websites, and other deceptive tactics. Realistic phishing simulations using AI can help employees become more vigilant and reduce the chances of falling for an attack.

Summary

Generative AI represents a double-edged sword in the world of cybersecurity. On the one hand, it offers powerful tools for improving threat detection, simulating attacks, and enhancing incident response. On the other hand, it introduces new threats, such as AI-driven malware, phishing, and social engineering attacks, that require novel defense strategies. The ethical considerations surrounding generative AI, including privacy, bias, and transparency issues, are also critical to address as this technology evolves. By leveraging the power of AI while implementing safeguards, organizations can harness its potential to improve cybersecurity while minimizing its risks.

Chapter 4: How AI Works in Cybersecurity

Introduction

In today's cybersecurity landscape, Artificial Intelligence (AI) is transforming how organizations defend against cyber threats. AI offers cutting-edge techniques for detecting, mitigating, and preventing various cyber risks. This chapter will delve into how AI functions within cybersecurity, focusing on key AI components such as machine learning (ML), natural language processing (NLP), neural networks, and deep learning. We will examine the algorithms central to AI-driven cybersecurity, explore how AI enhances traditional security frameworks, and discuss big data's pivotal role in reinforcing these defenses. Understanding how AI operates in cybersecurity provides valuable insight into its potential to strengthen security infrastructures and combat evolving cyber threats.

4.1 Machine Learning Basics

Machine learning (ML), a subset of AI, involves computers learning from data and improving their performance over time without being explicitly programmed. By detecting patterns and learning from examples, ML allows systems to make informed decisions. ML's primary role in cybersecurity is to identify anomalous behavior, detect malware, and continuously adapt to new attack patterns, enhancing system defenses.

Key components of machine learning in cybersecurity include:

- **Data Preprocessing**: Before training a model, data must be cleaned, transformed, and formatted for analysis. In cybersecurity, this involves removing noise from data and organizing it to highlight relevant patterns.

- **Training and Testing**: Machine learning models are trained on labeled data (supervised learning) or unlabeled data (unsupervised learning). The model learns patterns from the data and is later tested for its effectiveness.

- **Model Evaluation**: After training a model, its accuracy and performance are measured using metrics like precision, recall, and F1 score to assess its effectiveness in identifying threats.

Cybersecurity systems continuously improve by integrating ML, identifying emerging malware, phishing attempts, and sophisticated attack techniques. This adaptive nature makes machine learning a vital tool for modern cybersecurity.

4.2 Supervised, Unsupervised, and Reinforcement Learning

Machine learning can be broken down into three types, each suited for different challenges in cybersecurity. Understanding their distinctions and applications is essential for leveraging AI effectively.

Supervised Learning:

Supervised learning is a method where the model is trained on labeled data—each input is paired with the correct output. The model learns from these pairs to make predictions. In cybersecurity, this method is used for:

- **Spam Filtering**: Automatically classifying emails as legitimate or spam based on previously labeled examples.

- **Malware Detection**: Identifying known types of malware by matching input data with known malicious patterns.

Unsupervised Learning:

In unsupervised learning, the model is given data without labels and tasked with identifying underlying patterns or structures. This method is highly useful in cybersecurity for:

- **Anomaly Detection**: Identifying abnormal patterns, such as irregular user behavior or unknown cyberattacks, without relying on predefined data.

- **Cluster Analysis**: Grouping similar activities, such as identifying similar attack vectors or suspicious users in a network.

Reinforcement Learning:

Reinforcement learning focuses on learning through feedback—models adjust their actions based on rewards or penalties. This method can be applied to:

- **Automated Incident Response**: AI systems that adapt to past security incidents, adjusting defensive strategies based on the effectiveness of prior responses.

- **Dynamic Defense Strategies**: Reinforcement learning is useful for evolving threat landscapes, enabling AI to tweak security measures dynamically.

4.3 Natural Language Processing (NLP) in Cybersecurity

Natural Language Processing (NLP) enables machines to understand, interpret, and generate human language. In the realm of cybersecurity, NLP plays an essential role in parsing and analyzing large volumes of text data, such as security logs, emails, and threat intelligence feeds. Its key applications include:

Phishing Detection:

NLP algorithms can analyze email content for indicators of phishing attacks, such as suspicious language patterns, mismatched sender addresses, or deceptive phrasing. This enables automated detection of fraudulent emails before they reach end users.

Threat Intelligence Analysis:

To extract valuable threat intelligence, NLP processes unstructured textual data, including threat feeds, news reports, and social media content. By parsing massive amounts of raw data, NLP helps identify emerging attack tactics and provides actionable insights for security teams.

Incident Response Automation:

Using NLP, security systems can automatically process and categorize incident alerts or parse tickets. This reduces manual workload, speeds up decision-making, and accelerates the response to security events, improving operational efficiency.

Through NLP, AI enhances security teams' ability to process textual data quickly and efficiently, enabling faster detection of attacks and smoother incident response.

4.4 Neural Networks and Deep Learning

Neural networks are computational models inspired by the human brain's structure and functioning. They consist of layers of interconnected nodes (neurons) that process data inputs to generate meaningful outputs. Neural networks are the foundation of deep learning, a subset of machine learning that enables complex, high-level data analysis.

Deep Learning:

Deep learning models use neural networks with multiple layers to automatically extract complex features from large datasets. They excel in tasks involving large, unstructured data, such as:

- **Malware Detection**: By analyzing patterns in code or system behaviors, deep learning models can identify new types of malware that may not match known signatures.

- **Network Traffic Analysis**: These models can detect anomalies in network traffic, identifying potential threats like Distributed Denial of Service (DDoS) attacks or botnet activities.

- **Fraud Detection**: In financial cybersecurity, deep learning models detect abnormal transaction patterns indicative of fraudulent activity.

Deep learning enhances cybersecurity by enabling systems to learn from vast amounts of data autonomously, adapt to new threats, and continuously improve defenses.

4.5 AI Algorithms Used in Cybersecurity

Various AI algorithms are central to modern cybersecurity strategies. These algorithms help process data, identify patterns, and make informed decisions about security risks.

Decision Trees:

Decision trees break down decisions into a tree-like structure, where each node represents a decision based on input features. They are commonly used in:

- **Intrusion Detection**: Identifying network anomalies and classifying malicious traffic.

- **Malware Classification**: Categorizing malware based on known attack patterns.

Random Forests:

A random forest combines multiple decision trees, making the system more robust and accurate. It is widely used in:

- **Malware Classification**: By aggregating multiple decision trees, random forests improve accuracy in malware detection.

- **Intrusion Detection Systems (IDS)**: Enhancing the detection of sophisticated threats with higher precision.

Support Vector Machines (SVM):

SVM is a supervised learning algorithm used to classify data by finding the best separating hyperplane. It's effective for:

- **Spam Filtering**: Classifying email content as legitimate or spam.

- **Phishing Detection**: Identifying malicious websites and fraudulent communications.

K-Nearest Neighbors (KNN):

KNN is a simple yet effective algorithm that classifies data by comparing it to its nearest neighbors. In cybersecurity, KNN can be used for:

- **Intrusion Detection**: Detecting new attack vectors by comparing network traffic to known malicious patterns.

- **Pattern Recognition**: Identifying similar threats or behaviors based on past incidents.

4.6 AI-Powered Threat Intelligence Systems

AI-powered threat intelligence systems are transforming how organizations analyze and respond to emerging cybersecurity threats. These systems leverage big data analytics, machine learning, and real-time threat feeds to detect and mitigate risks.

Key benefits of AI-powered threat intelligence systems include:

- **Identifying New Attack Methods**: By analyzing vast amounts of attack data, AI can detect novel tactics and techniques used by cybercriminals, often before traditional security tools recognize them.

- **Prioritizing Threats**: AI helps categorize threats based on urgency, allowing security teams to focus on the most critical incidents that could have the greatest impact.

- **Automating Threat Detection and Response**: AI can flag

suspicious activities in real-time and initiate predefined responses, speeding up the mitigation process.

With AI-powered threat intelligence, organizations can move from a reactive to a proactive defense posture, improving the speed and accuracy of their cybersecurity operations.

4.7 The Role of Big Data in AI for Cybersecurity

Big data is the cornerstone of AI in cybersecurity, providing the vast amounts of structured and unstructured data needed for analysis. AI systems require access to large datasets to identify patterns, detect anomalies, and predict future risks.

Key aspects of big data in AI-driven cybersecurity include:

- **Data Volume**: AI systems need large datasets to train machine learning models effectively. The more data the model has, the better it can recognize patterns and predict threats.

- **Data Variety**: Cybersecurity data is diverse—ranging from network logs and transaction data to social media posts and threat intelligence feeds. AI can analyze all these data types to detect complex, multi-faceted threats.

- **Data Velocity**: AI-driven cybersecurity must process data in real-time to detect and respond to attacks as they happen. Big data tools enable rapid analysis, allowing systems to detect threats and take action instantly.

By utilizing big data, AI systems enhance threat detection accuracy and response times, providing a stronger defense against cyber risks.

4.8 Integrating AI with Traditional Security Models

While AI introduces advanced capabilities, integrating it with traditional security models is critical for comprehensive protection. Traditional security tools like firewalls, antivirus software, and intrusion detection systems form the backbone of cybersecurity. However, they are often static and struggle to keep pace with evolving threats.

Integrating AI with these tools provides significant benefits, including:

- **Enhanced Detection Capabilities**: AI improves the ability of traditional tools to identify unknown threats, filling in gaps where traditional models might fail.

- **Automated Response**: AI automates responses to certain types of attacks, speeding up remediation processes and reducing the burden on security teams.

- **Adaptive Security**: AI continuously learns from new data, allowing security systems to adapt to emerging threats and refine their detection and response strategies.

By combining AI with traditional security models, organizations can create a more robust, adaptive, and efficient defense system capable of addressing the full spectrum of modern cyber threats.

Summary

This chapter provided an in-depth look at how AI works in cybersecurity. We explored the various types of machine learning—supervised, unsupervised, and reinforcement learning—and their applications in detecting and responding to cyber threats. We also examined how natural language processing (NLP), neural networks, and deep learning enhance threat detection and analysis. Furthermore, we highlighted the importance of AI-powered threat intelligence systems and the role of big data in strengthening cybersecurity defenses. Finally, we discussed how integrating AI with traditional security models can optimize overall security effectiveness, allowing organizations to proactively detect, mitigate, and respond to a broad range of cyber threats.

Chapter 5: AI and Automation in Cybersecurity

Introduction

The increasing complexity and volume of cyber threats have outpaced the capabilities of traditional security measures. To counteract this challenge, automation and Artificial Intelligence (AI) have emerged as transformative tools in cybersecurity. Automation reduces human dependency on routine tasks, while AI enhances decision-making with intelligent insights. This chapter delves into the role of AI and automation in cybersecurity, exploring their applications, benefits, risks, and the necessity of human collaboration.

5.1 What Is Automation in Cybersecurity?

Definition and Significance:

Cybersecurity automation refers to deploying technologies that enable systems to carry out security tasks with minimal human intervention. The aim is to enhance efficiency, reduce response times, and improve accuracy in combating cyber threats. Automation is particularly effective in handling high-volume, repetitive tasks like log analysis, patch management, and incident reporting.

Common Use Cases of Automation in Cybersecurity:

1. **Vulnerability Scanning:** Automated tools proactively scan networks and applications for vulnerabilities, enabling timely remediation.

2. **Patch Management:** Systems automatically identify, download, and deploy software updates to mitigate risks.

3. **Security Information and Event Management (SIEM):** Automates collecting and analyzing security logs to detect anomalies and generate alerts.

4. **Compliance Monitoring:** Automation ensures continuous adherence to regulatory requirements by validating configurations and producing audit-ready reports.

Why Automation is Essential:

Manual processes are no longer sustainable with the ever-growing volume of cyber threats and data. Automation helps organizations address these challenges by increasing efficiency, consistency, and accuracy.

5.2 The Role of AI in Automating Security Tasks

AI enhances automation by introducing capabilities like machine learning, predictive analytics, and intelligent decision-making. These features allow automated systems to adapt and respond to emerging threats in real-time.

AI-Powered Capabilities in Security Automation:

- **Pattern Recognition:** AI models analyze vast datasets to identify malicious patterns or behaviors that human analysts might miss.
- **Adaptive Learning:** Machine learning algorithms continuously improve threat detection accuracy by learning from historical data.
- **Predictive Analytics:** AI predicts potential vulnerabilities or attack vectors, enabling proactive defense.

Examples of AI in Action:

1. **Threat Intelligence Analysis:** AI processes threat intelligence data to identify emerging risks.
2. **Behavioral Analysis:** AI detects deviations from normal user or system behavior to flag potential insider threats.
3. **Password Security:** AI tools identify weak or reused passwords and prompt users to strengthen them.

By integrating AI into automated processes, organizations achieve faster detection and response to cyber threats, reducing potential damage.

5.3 Automating Threat Detection and Response

Challenges in Traditional Threat Detection:

Traditional detection methods rely heavily on signature-based systems, which struggle to identify novel or polymorphic threats. Automated systems powered by AI address this limitation by employing advanced analytics and machine learning to detect even subtle anomalies.

Key Features of Automated Threat Detection:

- **Real-Time Monitoring:** Automated tools analyze data streams to detect threats as they occur.
- **Dynamic Anomaly Detection:** Machine learning models identify abnormal behaviors or patterns that could indicate an attack.
- **Intelligent Alerts:** AI reduces alert fatigue by prioritizing critical threats and filtering out false positives.

Automated Response Mechanisms:

Automation extends beyond detection to include responsive actions such as:

- **Quarantine:** Isolating infected devices to prevent lateral movement of malware.

- **Firewall Adjustments:** Automatically updating firewall rules to block malicious traffic.
- **Remediation Actions:** Executing pre-defined scripts to neutralize threats, such as removing malware or restoring backups.

5.4 AI-Powered Incident Response Systems

Incident response is critical to cybersecurity, where speed and accuracy are paramount. AI-powered systems streamline and enhance these processes, enabling faster and more effective responses to cyber incidents.

Core Components of AI-Powered Incident Response:

1. **Threat Identification:** AI systems analyze incoming data to categorize incidents and assess their severity.
2. **Automated Playbooks:** Pre-configured workflows guide systems to respond appropriately to various incident types.
3. **Root Cause Analysis:** AI identifies the origin of attacks, enabling targeted remediation.
4. **Data Correlation:** AI aggregates data from multiple sources to build a comprehensive picture of the incident.

Case in Point:

In a ransomware attack scenario, AI-powered systems can detect the anomaly, isolate affected devices, block further communication with the attacker, and initiate recovery procedures, all within minutes.

5.5 Benefits and Risks of Automation

Benefits of Automation:

1. **Enhanced Speed:** Automated systems process and respond to threats far faster than human analysts.

2. **Cost-Effectiveness:** Reduces the need for extensive manual labor, freeing resources for strategic activities.
3. **Consistency:** Ensures tasks are performed uniformly, reducing the risk of human error.
4. **Scalability:** Easily handles growing volumes of data and threats.
5. **Around-the-Clock Vigilance:** Automation enables 24/7 monitoring without fatigue.

Risks and Challenges:

1. **Over-Reliance:** Excessive dependence on automation may lead to vulnerabilities if systems fail or are bypassed.
2. **False Positives/Negatives:** Automated systems may misclassify threats, leading to unnecessary or missed responses.
3. **Complex Integration:** Adding automation to existing systems can be challenging and resource-intensive.
4. **Sophisticated Threats:** Attackers may exploit vulnerabilities in automated systems.

Mitigating these risks requires careful planning, continuous monitoring, and the inclusion of human oversight in automated processes.

5.6 Integrating AI with Existing Security Tools

Successful integration of AI with existing security infrastructure is key to realizing its full potential.

Steps for Seamless Integration:

1. **System Assessment:** Evaluate current tools and processes for compatibility with AI solutions.
2. **Centralized Data Management:** Consolidate data sources for streamlined AI analysis.
3. **Open APIs:** Ensure communication between AI systems and existing security tools using open APIs.

4. **Training:** Customize AI models to align with organizational security policies.

Real-World Integration Examples:

- **SIEM Tools:** AI enhances SIEM platforms by analyzing log data for actionable insights.
- **Firewalls:** AI dynamically adjusts firewall rules based on evolving threat intelligence.
- **Endpoint Security:** AI detects and mitigates endpoint vulnerabilities in real-time.

5.7 Case Study: Automation in Real-Time Cyber Threat Defense

Overview:

A multinational corporation with a large digital presence was facing persistent cybersecurity threats, including sophisticated phishing attacks and malware intrusions. Given the scale of its operations and the frequency of cyberattacks, the company was struggling to keep up with the ever-evolving threat landscape. Recognizing the need for more efficient and scalable security operations, the organization turned to Artificial Intelligence (AI) and automation technologies to improve its real-time cyber threat defense capabilities. The goal was to enhance threat detection, minimize the impact of breaches, and improve the efficiency of incident response.

Implementation Details:

1. **Automated Phishing Detection**:
   o The organization integrated Natural Language Processing (NLP) models into its email security systems to detect phishing attempts. These AI models were trained on vast datasets containing known phishing

patterns, suspicious phrases, and commonly used social engineering tactics.

o The NLP models scanned incoming emails for irregularities, including misleading sender information, suspicious subject lines, and unusual message content. When a potential phishing attempt was detected, the system automatically flagged the email as suspicious and quarantined it for further review. This process significantly reduced the risk of employees falling victim to phishing scams.

o Additionally, the AI system learned from ongoing threats and continuously adapted to new phishing techniques, improving detection accuracy over time.

2. **Malware Classification and Detection**:

o The company deployed machine learning (ML) algorithms to detect and classify malicious files that might slip past traditional antivirus solutions. Using supervised learning, these ML models were trained on large datasets of benign and malicious files, learning to identify subtle characteristics that distinguish harmful files from legitimate ones.

o Once integrated into the organization's endpoint security infrastructure, the AI system began to automatically scan files in real-time as they were downloaded, opened, or executed on the network. Suspicious files were immediately flagged, and the system used behavioral analysis to assess whether the file was attempting to exploit vulnerabilities or spread throughout the network.

o AI-driven malware classification allowed the security team to prioritize responses based on the severity and risk associated with each detected threat. Files deemed malicious were automatically quarantined, and further investigation was triggered based on the classification's confidence score.

3. **Incident Response Playbooks**:

   o To automate and expedite response actions, the company implemented Security Orchestration, Automation, and Response (SOAR) platforms. These platforms were used to define a series of automated incident response playbooks that could be triggered whenever a threat was detected.

   o For example, upon detection of a malware outbreak or an active phishing attempt, the SOAR platform could automatically isolate affected devices from the network, preventing the spread of the threat. This isolation was done by cutting off the device's network access and initiating automated remediation actions, such as patching vulnerable software or resetting user credentials.

   o The automated playbooks also included incident tracking, escalation protocols, and reporting mechanisms that kept the security operations center (SOC) team informed throughout the entire response process. This allowed the team to focus on high-priority incidents while routine tasks were handled by automation.

Outcome:

- **Incident Response Times Reduced by 70%**: The automation of detection and response workflows drastically cut down the time it took to identify and mitigate threats. Prior to implementing AI and automation, the response times to phishing attacks and malware intrusions could span hours or even days due to manual intervention. With automated systems in place, the company was able to address incidents within minutes, significantly reducing the window of opportunity for attackers to cause damage.

- **Phishing-Related Breaches Decreased by 90%**: By automating phishing detection using NLP, the company was able to catch phishing emails before they reached employees' inboxes. This led to a substantial reduction in phishing-related security incidents, with breaches related to these attacks dropping by 90%. Employees were also better educated on identifying phishing attempts, further strengthening the organization's defense.

- **Security Teams Reallocated Resources to Strategic Initiatives**: With AI handling routine threat detection and response actions, the security team was able to shift its focus from time-consuming, manual tasks to more strategic cybersecurity initiatives. Resources were allocated to improving security posture, conducting in-depth threat hunting, and developing new proactive security measures. The improved operational efficiency allowed the security team to focus on long-term goals, such as enhancing network segmentation and advancing threat intelligence strategies.

Conclusion:

This case study highlights the transformative power of AI and automation in modern cybersecurity defense. By incorporating machine learning, NLP, and SOAR platforms, the multinational corporation significantly enhanced its ability to detect and respond to threats in real-time. The result was a stronger security posture and a more efficient and scalable security operation. As the threat landscape continues to evolve, AI and automation will undoubtedly play an increasingly crucial role in enabling organizations to defend against cyberattacks more effectively.

5.8 The Human-AI Collaboration in Security Automation

Why Collaboration is Essential:

While automation and AI enhance efficiency, human expertise remains critical for nuanced decision-making, ethical oversight, and handling complex threats.

Roles of Humans in an Automated Environment:

- **Supervision:** Monitoring AI systems to ensure proper functioning.
- **Incident Analysis:** Investigating incidents that require contextual understanding.
- **Ethical Oversight:** Ensuring AI actions align with legal and ethical standards.

Examples of Collaboration:

- Security teams use AI-generated insights to prioritize and address high-risk vulnerabilities.
- Analysts refine AI models based on feedback from incident investigations.

Future of Human-AI Collaboration:

The future lies in symbiotic systems where humans and AI complement each other's strengths, building robust and adaptive cybersecurity defenses.

Summary

AI and automation are revolutionizing cybersecurity, offering unparalleled threat detection, response, and overall security management capabilities. However, these technologies are not without risks and challenges. By integrating automation with human expertise and existing tools, organizations can build a proactive and resilient defense against the ever-evolving cyber threat landscape.e Cases of AI in Cybersecurity

Artificial Intelligence (AI) has made significant strides in cybersecurity, offering innovative solutions to combat an ever-evolving landscape of cyber threats. By leveraging machine learning, natural language processing, and behavioral analytics, AI can automate tasks, detect anomalies, and predict potential risks in real-time, enhancing organizations' overall security posture. This chapter will delve into various practical use cases of AI in cybersecurity and how AI is shaping the future of digital security.

Chapter 6: Practical Use Cases of AI in Cybersecurity

Introduction

Artificial Intelligence (AI) has made remarkable strides in cybersecurity, transforming how organizations defend themselves against a growing array of sophisticated threats. From detecting cyberattacks in real-time to enhancing incident response capabilities, AI is playing an increasingly pivotal role in protecting systems and data. This chapter explores the various practical use cases of AI in cybersecurity, examining how AI-driven technologies revolutionize security operations.

6.1 AI for Threat Detection and Prevention

Overview

Traditional threat detection techniques often rely on known signatures and predefined rules to identify threats. However, AI-based systems use advanced machine learning (ML) algorithms to recognize new and emerging threats, which are often not detectable through traditional means.

How AI Works in Threat Detection

AI-driven threat detection systems process vast amounts of data from multiple sources, including network traffic, logs, and user activity. They analyze patterns and use predictive analytics to assess the likelihood of a potential attack. By continuously learning from past data, AI systems can identify both known and unknown threats, offering protection against zero-day attacks and sophisticated intrusion techniques.

Benefits of AI in Threat Prevention

AI's ability to recognize anomalies in real-time allows security teams to respond faster to emerging threats. The automation of threat detection significantly reduces the time spent manually reviewing alerts and enhances the overall efficiency of cybersecurity operations.

6.2 AI in Malware Analysis and Prevention

The Challenges of Traditional Malware Detection

Traditional malware detection systems often rely on signature-based detection methods, which require frequent updates to keep pace with new malware variants. This leaves organizations vulnerable to evolving threats.

AI-Driven Malware Analysis Techniques

AI enhances malware detection by analyzing file behavior, network activity, and execution patterns. Machine learning models are trained on large datasets of known malware samples and can detect unusual behaviors or characteristics in files and processes that may indicate the presence of malware.

Predictive Malware Prevention

Based on behavioral analysis and network activity, AI systems can also predict potential threats. This predictive ability allows AI to detect malware before it can execute, preventing widespread damage.

Outcome of AI in Malware Prevention

AI systems can provide a proactive defense against both known and unknown malware strains, reducing reliance on signature-based methods and improving the speed and accuracy of malware identification.

6.3 Phishing Detection and Prevention Using AI

Phishing Threats: A Growing Concern

Phishing attacks remain one of the most common and effective methods for cybercriminals to steal sensitive information. These attacks are often disguised as legitimate communications from trusted sources.

How AI Detects Phishing

AI-powered systems use Natural Language Processing (NLP) to analyze emails and other forms of communication for signs of phishing. AI can detect suspicious language patterns, such as urgency, threats, or enticing offers that are commonly used in phishing attempts. Additionally, machine learning algorithms examine URLs, attachments, and email metadata to identify fraudulent content.

Real-Time Phishing Prevention

AI-driven phishing detection systems can block phishing emails before they reach end-users, preventing malicious links and attachments from being clicked. Moreover, AI models can continuously learn from new phishing techniques, improving detection capabilities over time.

Case Study: Phishing Protection with AI

A **financial institution** facing increlasing phishing attacks decided to leverage AI to bolster its email security. Phishing, one of the most common types of cyberattacks, uses fraudulent emails to trick users into providing sensitive information such as login credentials account numbers, or even making wire transfers.

Implementation and Results:

- **AI-Driven Email Filtering**: The institution implemented an AI-powered email filtering system using machine learning models that were trained on vast datasets of historical phishing attempts. These models were capable of identifying common patterns in phishing emails, such as suspicious email addresses, manipulative language, and unexpected attachments or links.

- **Training the Model**: The system was trained using millions of examples of phishing and legitimate emails, including various forms of spear phishing, social engineering tactics, and common delivery methods.
- **Real-Time Detection**: The AI model was integrated with the organization's email infrastructure, providing real-time scanning of incoming emails. As a result, phishing emails were flagged before reaching employees' inboxes, significantly reducing the chances of employees engaging with malicious content.
- **Impact**: The deployment of this AI-driven filtering system led to a **90% reduction** in phishing-related breaches within the first year. Employees were less likely to fall victim to phishing attempts, significantly reducing the likelihood of account compromises, data breaches, and financial losses. Additionally, the financial institution was able to focus its resources on other areas of security, as the AI system handled the majority of phishing attacks automatically.

6.4 AI for Intrusion Detection Systems (IDS)

Intrusion Detection and Its Importance

Intrusion Detection Systems (IDS) are essential for identifying unauthorized access to network systems. Traditional IDS methods rely on signature-based detection, which may not be effective against new or sophisticated attack techniques.

How AI Enhances IDS

AI-powered IDS solutions use machine learning and anomaly detection algorithms to analyze real-time network traffic and system behavior. By detecting unusual patterns, such as unexpected login attempts or unauthorized access to sensitive data, AI can identify potential intrusions more quickly and accurately than traditional systems.

AI in Preventing False Positives

AI-driven IDS systems reduce false positives by continuously learning from past data. They can differentiate between benign anomalies and actual security threats, allowing security teams to focus on genuine risks while ignoring irrelevant alerts.

Case Study: AI for Advanced Intrusion Detection

A **major tech company** faced a growing concern over network security. With the complexity of its infrastructure and the rising sophistication of cyberattacks, traditional intrusion detection systems (IDS) were becoming increasingly ineffective. The company sought an AI-driven solution to bolster its defenses.

Implementation and Results:

- **AI-Powered IDS**: The tech company integrated an advanced AI-based IDS system that was designed to detect anomalous traffic patterns and unauthorized access attempts. The system employed deep learning and machine learning algorithms trained on large datasets containing network traffic from normal and attack scenarios.

- **Anomaly Detection**: The AI model could detect deviations from standard network behavior, such as unusual spikes in traffic, unusual access times, or anomalous traffic from unfamiliar locations. By focusing on patterns rather than predefined attack signatures, the system was able to identify novel threats, including zero-day exploits, without prior knowledge of the attack.

- **Real-Time Threat Response**: The system had a real-time response mechanism that could automatically block malicious traffic or alert security teams, depending on the severity of the threat. Over time, the AI system also improved its detection accuracy, becoming more efficient at identifying new attack

61

vectors.

- **Impact**: The AI-powered IDS led to a **50% reduction in security incidents** within the first six months. The company experienced fewer false positives, enabling security teams to focus on actual threats. This improvement enhanced the organization's overall network security, with faster identification and mitigation of security risks, reducing downtime and the potential for data breaches.

6.5 Using AI for Endpoint Security

The Growing Need for Endpoint Protection

As the number of devices connected to corporate networks continues to increase, securing endpoints such as computers, smartphones, and servers is crucial in preventing cyberattacks.

AI in Endpoint Detection and Response (EDR)

AI-powered Endpoint Detection and Response (EDR) systems use machine learning algorithms to analyze endpoints' behaviors and detect suspicious activity. These systems track file access, process interactions, and network connections to identify potential threats in real-time.

AI for Automated Endpoint Remediation

AI-driven systems can also automate the process of endpoint remediation. Once a threat is detected, AI systems can isolate the infected endpoint, block malicious processes, and even remove malware automatically, reducing the response time and minimizing damage.

Outcome of AI in Endpoint Security

By leveraging AI, organizations can improve endpoint security through real-time detection, automated response, and continuous learning, enhancing protection against both known and unknown threats.

6.6 AI-Powered SIEM (Security Information and Event Management)

Traditional SIEM vs. AI-Powered SIEM

Traditional SIEM systems rely on predefined rules and human analysts to correlate and analyze security events. This process can be time-consuming and prone to errors.

How AI Enhances SIEM Capabilities

AI-powered SIEM systems use machine learning algorithms to automate the process of data correlation and threat detection. These systems can analyze vast amounts of security event data from multiple sources, such as firewalls, intrusion detection systems, and servers, to detect potential security incidents.

Real-Time Threat Detection with AI-Driven SIEM

AI enhances SIEM by automating the identification and prioritization of security incidents. Machine learning models analyze historical data and use predictive analytics to identify emerging threats, reducing the time it takes to detect and respond to attacks.

Case Study: SIEM System Implementation with AI

A **large healthcare provider** with a complex IT environment sought to improve its security information and event management (SIEM) system. The goal was to enhance its ability to detect and respond to security incidents in real-time, while ensuring compliance with healthcare data privacy regulations such as HIPAA.

Implementation and Results:

- **AI-Enhanced SIEM**: The healthcare provider integrated an AI-powered SIEM system designed to process and analyze vast amounts of security data from across its network. The AI system used machine learning algorithms to correlate and detect potential security incidents by identifying real-time patterns, anomalies, and potential threats.

- **Automation of Incident Response**: The AI system was integrated with the healthcare provider's security infrastructure to automate incident detection, prioritize threats, and trigger predefined response protocols. This minimized the response time and allowed the security team to focus on higher-priority tasks.

- **Enhanced Threat Intelligence**: The AI model continuously learned from new data, improving its ability to identify emerging threats. It could also cross-reference external threat intelligence feeds to detect known indicators of compromise (IoCs) or tactics, techniques, and procedures (TTPs) associated with cyberattacks.

- **Impact**: The AI-powered SIEM system helped the healthcare provider **reduce response times by 60%**, allowing the security team to quickly address critical threats. The system also improved incident detection accuracy, reducing the number of false alarms and enhancing the provider's ability to prevent potential breaches and ensure regulatory compliance.

6.7 Behavioral Analytics and AI for Insider Threat Detection

The Challenge of Insider Threats

Insider threats, whether malicious or unintentional, can cause significant damage to an organization. Detecting these threats can be challenging because insiders typically have legitimate access to systems and data.

AI and Behavioral Analytics in Insider Threat Detection

AI uses behavioral analytics to monitor employee activity and detect deviations from normal behavior. By analyzing factors such as login times, access patterns, and communication behavior, AI can identify potential insider threats, including those caused by compromised credentials.

Case Study: AI for Insider Threat Detection

A **financial institution** was concerned about the increasing threat of insider attacks, where employees or contractors might misuse access to sensitive data or systems. The institution implemented an AI-driven behavioral analytics system to monitor employee activities and detect anomalous behavior indicative of potential insider threats.

Implementation and Results:

- **Behavioral Analytics with AI**: The financial institution deployed an AI system that continuously monitored employee behavior within its network. The system used machine learning algorithms to analyze access patterns, data usage, login times, and other activity data.

- **Identifying Unusual Behavior**: The AI system flagged abnormal activities, such as accessing sensitive data outside of normal working hours, accessing files unrelated to an employee's role, or downloading large volumes of data without justification. This helped security teams detect potential signs of insider threats, including data theft or privilege abuse.

- **Real-Time Monitoring**: The AI system continuously learned from employee behavior, refining its model to identify new and evolving patterns of suspicious activities. Alerts were generated for security teams when anomalies were detected, triggering further investigation.

- **Impact**: The implementation of AI-driven behavioral analytics helped the financial institution identify and prevent several potential insider threats. The system was able to catch subtle, abnormal behavior that might have otherwise gone unnoticed, reducing the risk of data breaches and protecting sensitive financial data.

6.8 Fraud Detection with AI

Fraud in Financial Services

Fraud remains a significant concern in financial transactions, with cybercriminals using increasingly sophisticated techniques to exploit vulnerabilities in payment systems.

AI in Fraud Detection

AI-powered fraud detection systems use machine learning algorithms to analyze transaction data in real-time. These systems learn from historical transaction data to identify abnormal patterns, such as irregular payment amounts or transactions originating from suspicious locations.

Predictive Fraud Prevention

By using predictive analytics, AI systems can detect potential fraud before it occurs, allowing organizations to take preventive action and block fraudulent transactions in real-time.

Case Study: AI-Driven Fraud Detection

An **e-commerce company** wanted to enhance its ability to detect and prevent fraudulent transactions on its platform. With millions of transactions processed daily, manual review methods were no longer feasible, and traditional fraud detection tools were often overwhelmed by false positives.

Implementation and Results:

- **AI-Based Fraud Detection**: The e-commerce company implemented an AI-based fraud detection system that utilized machine learning algorithms to analyze transaction data in real-time. The system was trained on historical transaction data, including fraudulent and legitimate purchases, and learned to identify features that correlated with fraud, such as unusual purchase behavior or geographic anomalies.

- **Adaptive Learning**: The AI system was capable of adapting to new fraud patterns as it processed more data. By identifying subtle patterns in user behavior, the system could flag suspicious transactions before they were processed.

- **Transaction Blocking**: The system could block flagged transactions automatically or alert human reviewers for further investigation. The AI model also helped prioritize which transactions needed manual review, improving the efficiency of fraud investigation.

- **Impact**: The implementation of AI for fraud detection resulted in a **40% reduction in fraud**. The system helped the company prevent significant financial losses, protect its customers, and reduce the number of false positives that previously required manual review. The automation also improved the customer experience by reducing the number of false alarms.

6.9 Case Study: AI for Data Privacy and Compliance in Cybersecurity

The Importance of Data Privacy and Compliance

As data privacy regulations such as GDPR and CCPA become more stringent, organizations must ensure that they comply with these laws while safeguarding personal data.

AI in Data Privacy and Compliance

AI can automate the process of data classification and ensure that personal data is encrypted and securely stored. Machine learning algorithms can identify sensitive data across vast datasets, allowing organizations to maintain compliance with data privacy regulations.

Case Study: Automating Data Privacy with AI

A **global healthcare provider** faced increasing pressure to comply with strict data privacy regulations like GDPR and HIPAA. The organization needed an efficient way to classify and manage sensitive data while automating responses to potential privacy breaches.

Implementation and Results:

- **AI-Powered Data Classification**: The healthcare provider implemented an AI-driven data privacy system that used machine learning models to classify and categorize sensitive data. The system could automatically identify and tag data such as personally identifiable information (PII), medical records, and financial information.

- **Regulatory Compliance Automation**: The AI system also helped automate privacy compliance tasks, including ensuring data was properly anonymized, stored securely, and accessed only by authorized personnel. The system used machine learning models to assess data access requests and flag any potentially non-compliant activities.

- **Risk Mitigation**: By automating compliance monitoring and data management, the AI system minimized non-compliance risk and helped the organization maintain continuous adherence to regulatory standards.

- **Impact**: The AI-driven data privacy system enabled the healthcare provider to significantly reduce manual efforts required for compliance tasks, minimize the risk of privacy violations, and enhance customer trust by demonstrating a commitment to data security and privacy.

6.10 AI in the Protection of Critical Infrastructure

Securing Critical Infrastructure

Critical infrastructure systems, such as energy grids and transportation networks, are vital to national security and require robust cybersecurity measures to protect them from cyberattacks.

AI for Real-Time Monitoring and Threat Detection

AI-powered systems continuously monitor critical infrastructure for signs of cyberattacks or system failures. Machine learning algorithms analyze data from various sources, such as sensors and control systems, to detect anomalies that may indicate an attack or malfunction.

Predictive Maintenance with AI

AI also enhances critical infrastructure protection by predicting potential failures and enabling predictive maintenance. By analyzing historical data and current system conditions, AI can forecast when equipment is likely to fail, allowing for preventive actions to be taken before a failure occurs.

Case Study: AI in Critical Infrastructure Protection

A **national power grid** responsible for the distribution of electricity across a large region sought to protect its critical infrastructure from cyberattacks. The organization turned to AI to enhance its defense capabilities as cyber threats became more advanced.

Implementation and Results:

- **AI for Cybersecurity Monitoring**: The power grid implemented an AI system that monitored its critical infrastructure for signs of cyberattacks. The AI model analyzed data from various sources, such as network traffic, control system logs, and external threat intelligence feeds.

- **Detection of Abnormal Traffic Patterns**: The AI system uses machine learning algorithms to detect abnormal traffic patterns, such as unauthorized access attempts or unusual communications within the grid's network. The system could also identify attempts to manipulate operational data or disrupt system performance.

- **Real-Time Incident Response**: The AI system automatically triggered alerts and initiated countermeasures when potential attacks were detected. It also coordinated responses with human security teams for more complex incidents.

- **Impact:** The AI-powered cybersecurity system successfully detected and prevented several attempts to breach the power grid's infrastructure, ensuring its continuous operation. The system's real-time detection and response capabilities helped protect critical infrastructure from emerging threats and minimized the risk of a potentially catastrophic attack.

Summary

AI has become a powerful ally in the battle against cyber threats, enabling organizations to detect and mitigate risks more effectively than ever before. From enhancing malware analysis to automating incident response, AI is transforming the way organizations approach cybersecurity. By leveraging the power of AI, organizations can not only respond more swiftly to attacks but also proactively defend against emerging threats, ultimately strengthening their security posture in an increasingly complex digital landscape. As AI continues to evolve, its role in cybersecurity will only expand, offering even greater protection for systems, data, and critical infrastructure.

Chapter 7: Relevant AI Models for Cybersecurity

Introduction

Artificial Intelligence (AI) has become an integral part of modern cybersecurity. The speed at which cyber threats evolve and the increasing sophistication of these threats make traditional, manual methods of defense inadequate. AI, particularly through machine learning (ML), deep learning (DL), natural language processing (NLP), and reinforcement learning (RL), offers advanced solutions to detect, prevent, and mitigate these threats. In this chapter, we will dive deeper into the different AI models used in cybersecurity, examining their roles, applications, and performance in real-world scenarios.

7.1 Overview of AI Models Used in Cybersecurity

AI models in cybersecurity are designed to analyze large volumes of data, detect anomalies, and adapt to new, emerging threats. They can work in a variety of contexts—from monitoring network traffic to identifying malware to automating incident response. The main types of AI models employed in cybersecurity are:

- **Machine Learning (ML)**: Includes both supervised and unsupervised learning. These models learn patterns from data to classify, predict, and identify anomalies.

- **Deep Learning (DL)**: A subset of ML that involves neural networks with multiple layers. Deep learning is particularly adept at handling complex, high-dimensional data like images and network traffic.

- **Natural Language Processing (NLP)**: Allows systems to understand and generate human language, which is useful in analyzing security logs, email contents, and communication.

- **Reinforcement Learning (RL)**: Focuses on training systems to make decisions by interacting with an environment and optimizing actions based on rewards or penalties.

These models are employed across various areas of cybersecurity, including threat detection, incident response, and fraud prevention, making them essential tools in the fight against cybercrime.

7.2 Machine Learning Models for Threat Detection

Machine learning has revolutionized threat detection by automating the analysis of massive datasets and uncovering hidden patterns that might go unnoticed by traditional systems. ML models are increasingly used to identify and block threats in real-time.

Supervised Learning

Supervised learning involves training a model on labeled data where both the input (features) and the output (labels) are provided. The model learns a mapping function from the input to the output and uses this knowledge to predict outcomes for new, unseen data.

Applications in Cybersecurity:

- **Malware Detection**: In supervised learning, algorithms are trained to distinguish between benign and malicious files based on features such as file size, file type, and signature.
- **Intrusion Detection Systems (IDS)**: Supervised learning can classify network traffic as normal or anomalous based on patterns from previously labeled data, helping to detect potential intrusions in real-time.

- **Phishing Detection**: Supervised learning models can be trained to detect phishing emails by analyzing specific features like the sender's address, subject line, language, and links within the message.

Challenges:

- Requires large, high-quality labeled datasets for accurate predictions.
- Can struggle with overfitting if the model is too complex or the dataset is too small.

Unsupervised Learning

Unsupervised learning, in contrast, works with unlabeled data. The model tries to find structure or patterns in the data without prior knowledge of the categories or labels. It is particularly useful for anomaly detection and discovering new, previously unseen threats.

Applications in Cybersecurity:

- **Anomaly Detection**: Unsupervised learning can detect unusual patterns in network traffic, which might indicate a new form of attack, such as a Distributed Denial of Service (DDoS) attack or a botnet activity.
- **Zero-Day Exploits**: Since the model isn't trained on known threats, unsupervised learning is valuable in identifying new types of attacks that don't match established patterns or signatures.

Challenges:

- May produce more false positives than supervised models, as it lacks the context provided by labeled data.
- Often, it requires careful tuning to avoid incorrect conclusions.

7.3 Deep Learning Models in Cyber Defense

Deep learning is an advanced branch of machine learning that uses neural networks with multiple hidden layers. These models are particularly effective at handling large and unstructured datasets, such as images videos, and complex time-series data like network traffic or security logs.

How Deep Learning Works

Deep learning models are designed to automatically learn and extract features from raw data, reducing the need for manual feature engineering. The more layers in a neural network, the more complex patterns it can learn.

Applications in Cybersecurity:

- **Malware Classification**: DL models are used to analyze file contents, metadata, and behavioral patterns to detect and classify previously unknown malware, including polymorphic and metamorphic malware.

- **Behavioral Analysis**: By learning patterns of normal systems or user behavior, deep learning can detect anomalies that might indicate insider threats, account compromise, or privilege escalation.

- **Network Traffic Analysis**: Deep learning models are ideal for analyzing high-volume network traffic, identifying suspicious behavior, and distinguishing between benign and malicious traffic.

Advantages:

- Capable of automating complex decision-making processes.

- Able to learn from vast amounts of data, improving accuracy over time.

Challenges:

- Requires large datasets and significant computational resources to train.

- Often described as "black-box" models, making it difficult to interpret how decisions are made, which can be problematic for transparency in cybersecurity operations.

7.4 Natural Language Processing Models for Security

Natural Language Processing (NLP) allows computers to process and understand human language, an essential capability in many cybersecurity applications. NLP is particularly useful for analyzing text data such as emails, security logs, and chat messages, which often contain critical information regarding potential threats.

NLP Techniques in Cybersecurity:

- **Text Classification**: NLP can classify text as malicious or benign by analyzing words, phrases, and context, helping to detect phishing emails, spam, and social engineering attacks.
- **Sentiment Analysis**: Sentiment analysis can be used to detect potential threats in customer support messages, forum posts, or emails. For example, employees might use NLP to identify hostile or suspicious language in communication with clients or other internal actors.
- **Named Entity Recognition (NER)**: NER can identify and extract entities like domain names, IP addresses, and user credentials from unstructured text, helping security teams track indicators of compromise (IoCs).

Applications in Cybersecurity:

- **Phishing Detection**: NLP models can examine emails' language, grammar, and contextual cues to identify phishing attempts. They can also detect the use of malicious URLs or attachments.

- **Security Log Analysis**: Analyzing verbose and technical log files can be challenging, but NLP models help parse these logs and identify critical security events, such as failed login attempts or unusual system activity.

Advantages:

- Can process large amounts of unstructured text data in real-time.
- Effective at detecting social engineering and phishing attacks.

Challenges:

- NLP models require substantial training data to handle various languages and contexts.
- Contextual understanding may be difficult if the text is ambiguous or uses unfamiliar terminology.

7.5 Reinforcement Learning in Cybersecurity

Reinforcement Learning (RL) is a type of machine learning where an agent learns by interacting with an environment and receiving feedback based on its actions. This feedback is in the form of rewards (positive feedback) or penalties (negative feedback). RL is particularly effective for tasks where sequential decision-making is required.

How Reinforcement Learning Works

RL models consist of an agent, a set of actions, and a reward system. The agent learns to optimize its actions over time to maximize cumulative rewards. In cybersecurity, RL can be used to train systems to respond to security events dynamically, improving defense mechanisms based on feedback.

Applications in Cybersecurity:

- **Automated Incident Response**: RL can automate security decisions such as isolating infected devices or blocking malicious traffic in real-time. The system learns from previous security incidents to take the most effective action in future attacks.
- **Penetration Testing**: RL simulates and optimizes attack strategies in penetration testing, allowing organizations to identify vulnerabilities and test their defenses in a controlled manner.

Advantages:

- Can adapt to changing threat landscapes and optimize defense strategies.
- Able to make dynamic decisions in complex environments with high variability.

Challenges:

- Requires a well-defined reward system and environment for training.
- Training can be resource-intensive and time-consuming.

7.6 Case Study: AI Model Performance in Real-World Scenarios

Case Study Overview

This case study explores the use of AI models in a financial institution that faced increasing threats of fraud, phishing, and insider attacks. The organization deployed a combination of machine learning, deep learning, and reinforcement learning models to enhance its cybersecurity infrastructure.

Key Models Implemented:

- **Supervised Learning**: Used for phishing detection by training a model to classify email communication based on known phishing techniques.
- **Deep Learning**: Employed to detect anomalous transaction patterns and classify transactions as legitimate or fraudulent.
- **Reinforcement Learning**: Applied to adjust network defense mechanisms based on real-time threat detection automatically.

Results:

- Fraud detection accuracy improved by 30% over traditional methods.
- Incident response time was reduced by 40% due to automated defense systems powered by RL.
- The institution successfully identified and thwarted multiple zero-day exploits using unsupervised anomaly detection.

7.7 Exploring the Effectiveness of AI Models in Adapting to New Threats

AI models in cybersecurity must be capable of adapting to the fast-changing landscape of cyber threats. These models, particularly those based on machine learning and reinforcement learning, can continuously learn from new data, allowing them to respond effectively to novel threats.

Continuous Adaptation:

- **Real-Time Learning**: AI models can be trained to learn from new data as it becomes available, allowing them to detect and mitigate emerging threats faster than traditional methods.
- **Self-Tuning**: Models can be designed to automatically tune their parameters to optimize performance, adjusting to new threat types without human intervention.

Challenges:

- As cybercriminals evolve their techniques, AI models may require frequent retraining to stay effective.
- Ensuring the models don't overfit specific data patterns is crucial for maintaining generalization across various types of attacks.

7.8 Balancing Accuracy and Performance in AI Models for Cybersecurity

AI models for cybersecurity face the challenge of balancing accuracy with real-time performance. While high accuracy is desirable for detecting threats, it often comes at the cost of processing speed, especially when handling large datasets in real-time environments.

Key Considerations:

- **False Positives vs. False Negatives**: High accuracy typically reduces false negatives (missed threats) but may increase false positives, which can overwhelm security teams. Striking the right balance between these two is crucial.
- **Real-Time Detection**: Performance (speed) is often prioritized over absolute accuracy for systems that need to react in real-time. The challenge is to identify critical threats quickly while minimizing the computational cost.

Solutions:

- **Hybrid Models**: Combining multiple AI techniques (e.g., supervised learning for known threats and unsupervised learning for unknown threats) can help balance accuracy and performance.
- **Model Compression and Optimization**: Techniques like pruning or quantization can make deep learning models more efficient without sacrificing too much accuracy.

Summary

AI models are pivotal in modern cybersecurity. Their ability to detect and respond to threats faster and more accurately than traditional systems is crucial in today's digital landscape. As AI technologies evolve, they will continue to enhance the ability of organizations to protect their assets and data from a growing range of sophisticated cyber threats. However, challenges such as model interpretability, data quality, and resource requirements remain, and addressing these will be key to the widespread adoption and success of AI in cybersecurity.

Chapter 8: Practical AI Codes for Cybersecurity

Introduction

This chapter will explore the practical applications of artificial intelligence (AI) in cybersecurity. The focus will be on essential programming languages, libraries, and step-by-step guides on building AI models for various security tasks. Additionally, we'll delve into troubleshooting, optimizing AI models, and how to integrate AI into existing security infrastructures, which is critical for enhancing real-time threat detection and response.

8.1 Overview of Key Programming Languages in AI

In the context of AI for cybersecurity, the choice of programming language plays a pivotal role in determining the ease of development, the availability of libraries, and overall performance. Let's delve deeper into the key programming languages used in AI development:

Python

Python remains the de facto language for AI due to its simplicity, flexibility, and strong support for machine learning (ML) and deep learning (DL) frameworks. Python is particularly popular for implementing AI in cybersecurity because:

- **Extensive Libraries**: Python has an ecosystem full of libraries like **TensorFlow, Keras, PyTorch, Scikit-learn,** and **NLTK** for developing AI models tailored to cybersecurity tasks, such as phishing detection, anomaly detection, and malware analysis.

- **Community Support**: Python boasts a large and active community that continuously develops and maintains a plethora of open-source tools, making it easy to integrate new techniques into your AI solutions.

R

While R is primarily used for data analysis and statistics, it also plays a role in AI for cybersecurity, particularly in **data mining** and **predictive analytics**. R excels at:

- **Statistical Modeling**: It is highly efficient in performing statistical analysis on large datasets to uncover hidden patterns or trends that could represent cybersecurity threats.
- **Visualization**: R's data visualization libraries (like **ggplot2**) allow for easy interpretation of security-related data, such as identifying trends in attack patterns.

Java

Java's **scalability** and **platform independence** make it a robust choice for large-scale enterprise cybersecurity applications. It is often used for:

- **Building Security Applications**: Java is ideal for developing complex, high-performance cybersecurity applications such as **firewalls**, **IDS/IPS**, and **SIEM systems** that need to run in large enterprise environments.
- **Real-time Detection**: Java can process data in real-time, which is essential for cybersecurity scenarios that require quick decision-making and threat mitigation.

C++

C++ provides low-level access to hardware and is therefore valuable in real-time security applications, such as:

- **Real-Time Intrusion Detection**: C++ is often employed when real-time processing of large amounts of network data is crucial, ensuring that AI models can function at optimal speed without delays.
- **Memory Management**: C++ offers fine control over memory usage, making it useful in applications with strict performance requirements like anomaly detection systems.

8.2 Implementing AI in Cybersecurity: A Step-by-Step Guide

This section provides practical implementations of AI in cybersecurity. We will focus on building AI models for **intrusion detection** and **malware detection** using Python.

Building a Basic Intrusion Detection System with Machine Learning

Intrusion Detection Systems (IDS) are designed to monitor network traffic for signs of suspicious activity, such as unauthorized access or abnormal behavior. Let's break down the steps to build a basic machine learning-based IDS.

1. **Data Collection**: We can use the **KDD Cup 1999 dataset**, which contains a variety of attacks and normal network traffic.
2. **Preprocessing**: Preprocessing network traffic data involves encoding categorical data, normalizing numerical features, and splitting the data into training and testing sets.

```python
python
```

```
import pandas as pd
from sklearn.preprocessing import LabelEncoder
from sklearn.model_selection import train_test_split
from sklearn.ensemble import RandomForestClassifier

# Load and clean data
data = pd.read_csv('kddcup.data_10_percent.csv')
data.fillna(method='ffill', inplace=True)

# Label encoding for categorical variables
label_encoder = LabelEncoder()
data['protocol_type'] =
label_encoder.fit_transform(data['protocol_type'])

X = data.drop('class', axis=1)
y = data['class']

# Split data
X_train, X_test, y_train, y_test = train_test_split(X, y,
test_size=0.3, random_state=42)
```

3. **Training the Model**: For simplicity, we can use **Random Forest** for binary classification to detect normal vs. attack traffic.

```python
rf_model = RandomForestClassifier(n_estimators=100)
rf_model.fit(X_train, y_train)
```

4. **Evaluation**: We evaluate the model's accuracy using standard metrics like accuracy, precision, recall, and F1-score.

```python
```

```
from sklearn.metrics import classification_report

y_pred = rf_model.predict(X_test)
print(classification_report(y_test, y_pred))
```

Result: The model can now predict whether network traffic is malicious or benign based on the KDD dataset.

Implementing Malware Detection Using Neural Networks

For malware detection, we will build a deep learning model that classifies executable files as either malicious or benign. This model can analyze files based on features like byte sequences, system calls, and network behavior.

1. **Data Collection**: We can use the **Microsoft Malware Classification Challenge** dataset or similar data, which contains features derived from malware samples.
2. **Preprocessing**: Files need to be transformed into numeric data (e.g., byte sequences) that can be input to a neural network.

```python
python

from tensorflow.keras.preprocessing import sequence

# Preprocessing to normalize and reshape the data
data = pd.read_csv('malware_data.csv')
X = data.drop('label', axis=1)
y = data['label']

X_scaled = sequence.pad_sequences(X, maxlen=100)  # Pad to
consistent length
```

3. **Building a Neural Network**: Use TensorFlow to build a deep neural network that can learn the patterns indicative of malware.

```python
from tensorflow.keras.models import Sequential
from tensorflow.keras.layers import Dense, Dropout

model = Sequential()
model.add(Dense(128, input_dim=X_scaled.shape[1], activation='relu'))
model.add(Dropout(0.5))
model.add(Dense(1, activation='sigmoid'))

model.compile(optimizer='adam', loss='binary_crossentropy', metrics=['accuracy'])
model.fit(X_scaled, y, epochs=10, batch_size=32)
```

4. **Evaluation**: Evaluate the model's performance on test data to determine its ability to classify malware.

```python
test_loss, test_acc = model.evaluate(X_test, y_test)
print(f'Test accuracy: {test_acc}')
```

Result: The deep learning model will classify files as benign or malware, potentially aiding in automatically detecting new malware variants.

8.3 Python Libraries for AI in Cybersecurity

Several Python libraries are central to building AI models for cybersecurity. Here's a closer look at these libraries and how they can be leveraged:

TensorFlow and Keras

- **TensorFlow** is a comprehensive open-source platform for machine learning. It is highly suitable for deploying deep learning models at scale and is widely used in AI-powered security applications such as intrusion detection, malware analysis, and fraud detection.
- **Keras** is a high-level neural networks API that runs on top of TensorFlow, making experimenting with deep learning models easier.

```python
import tensorflow as tf
from tensorflow.keras.models import Sequential
from tensorflow.keras.layers import Dense
```

PyTorch

PyTorch offers greater flexibility than TensorFlow and is widely used in research and development for AI-based cybersecurity systems. It supports dynamic computation graphs, which makes it suitable for applications that require flexible and fast iterations.

```python
import torch
import torch.nn as nn
```

Scikit-learn

Scikit-learn is ideal for traditional machine learning models (e.g., decision trees, random forests, support vector machines) and is widely used for classification tasks in cybersecurity, such as identifying attack types and detecting phishing emails.

```
python

from sklearn.ensemble import RandomForestClassifier
from sklearn.metrics import accuracy_score
```

NLTK and SpaCy for NLP

Natural Language Processing (NLP) is critical for analyzing textual data in phishing emails, threat intelligence feeds, and other unstructured data sources. **NLTK** and **SpaCy** are two leading Python libraries for processing text.

```
python

import nltk
import spacy
```

8.4 Example Codes: AI for Threat Detection, Phishing, and Malware Analysis

Artificial Intelligence has become an indispensable tool in cybersecurity, enabling organizations to automate complex tasks such as phishing detection, malware analysis, and threat identification. Here are detailed examples of how AI can be applied in these domains.

AI for Phishing Detection

Phishing detection focuses on identifying fraudulent attempts to steal sensitive information, often through emails. Machine learning models like Naive Bayes and Support Vector Machines (SVM) can analyze email content to detect suspicious patterns.

Python Example: Naive Bayes for Phishing Detection

```
python
```

```
from sklearn.feature_extraction.text import CountVectorizer
from sklearn.naive_bayes import MultinomialNB

# Sample email data
emails = [
    "Congratulations, you have won $1,000! Click here to claim your
prize.",
    "Please confirm your bank account number for security verification.",
    "Meeting at 3 PM tomorrow in the conference room.",
    "Your invoice is attached. Let us know if you have any questions."
]
labels = [1, 1, 0, 0]  # 1: Phishing, 0: Legitimate

# Convert text data to numerical format
vectorizer = CountVectorizer()
X = vectorizer.fit_transform(emails)

# Train a Naive Bayes model
model = MultinomialNB()
model.fit(X, labels)

# Test the model
test_email = ["Urgent: Update your account information now."]
test_vectorized = vectorizer.transform(test_email)
prediction = model.predict(test_vectorized)
print(f"Prediction: {'Phishing' if prediction[0] == 1 else 'Legitimate'}")
```

AI for Malware Detection

Malware detection involves classifying software as malicious or benign based on its characteristics. Machine learning models, such as Random Forests or Deep Neural Networks, are commonly used for this purpose.

Python Example: Random Forest for Malware Detection

```python
python

from sklearn.ensemble import RandomForestClassifier
from sklearn.model_selection import train_test_split
from sklearn.metrics import classification_report

# Example dataset (features and labels)
X = [[0.1, 0.3, 0.5], [0.9, 0.8, 0.7], [0.2, 0.2, 0.1], [0.6, 0.6, 0.5]]  # Features
(e.g., extracted from binary files)
y = [1, 1, 0, 0]  # 1: Malware, 0: Benign

# Split data into training and testing sets
X_train, X_test, y_train, y_test = train_test_split(X, y, test_size=0.3,
random_state=42)

# Train a Random Forest model
model = RandomForestClassifier(n_estimators=100, random_state=42)
model.fit(X_train, y_train)

# Test the model
y_pred = model.predict(X_test)
print("Classification Report:")
print(classification_report(y_test, y_pred))
```

8.5 Integrating AI Models into Security Infrastructure

To fully leverage AI in cybersecurity, integration into existing security systems is essential. Below are some key strategies for effective integration:

APIs for Model Deployment

- **Expose AI Models**: Use REST APIs to deploy AI models, making them accessible to other security systems, such as firewalls and Security Information and Event Management (SIEM) platforms.

- **Example Frameworks**: Frameworks like Flask, FastAPI, or Django can be used to serve AI models.

Automation with AI

- **Automated Responses**: Configure the system to take immediate actions, such as blocking malicious IPs or isolating compromised devices, based on AI model predictions.
- **Playbooks and Orchestration**: Leverage platforms like SOAR (Security Orchestration, Automation, and Response) for automating workflows.

Continuous Monitoring and Updates

- **Real-Time Data Streams**: Integrate with real-time data sources (e.g., Syslog, SNMP, or network telemetry) to ensure models remain updated.
- **Adaptive Learning**: Implement continuous learning pipelines to adapt models to evolving threats.

8.6 Troubleshooting and Optimizing AI Models for Cybersecurity

AI models in cybersecurity require regular optimization to maintain accuracy and efficiency. Below are best practices to troubleshoot and optimize these models:

Hyperparameter Tuning

- Use methods like **Grid Search** or **Random Search** to find optimal hyperparameters (e.g., learning rates, number of trees, dropout rates).
- Example:

```
python

from sklearn.model_selection import GridSearchCV

param_grid = {'n_estimators': [50, 100, 150], 'max_depth': [10,
20, None]}
grid_search    =    GridSearchCV(RandomForestClassifier(),
param_grid, cv=3)
grid_search.fit(X_train, y_train)
print(grid_search.best_params_)
```

Cross-Validation

- Implement **k-fold cross-validation** to test model robustness and avoid overfitting.

Feature Engineering

- Extract domain-specific features like network packet sizes, HTTP headers, or executable metadata to improve model relevance.
- Tools like pandas and numpy can assist in feature extraction and preprocessing.

Model Evaluation

- Evaluate models using metrics like:
  - **Precision and Recall**: Measure the model's ability to avoid false positives and false negatives.
  - **F1-Score**: Ensure a balance between precision and recall.
  - **ROC-AUC**: Assess the trade-off between true positive and false positive rates.

8.7 Cloud-Based AI Code Execution for Cybersecurity

Cloud platforms provide scalable environments to execute AI models and handle large-scale cybersecurity tasks. Below are some examples:

AWS SageMaker

- Train and deploy AI models using SageMaker's built-in algorithms and managed infrastructure.
- Example: Integrate SageMaker with Amazon S3 to store training data and use AWS Lambda for automated responses.

Azure Machine Learning

- Use Azure ML to build and deploy machine learning pipelines, leveraging Azure Security Center for threat management.

Google Cloud AI

- Deploy TensorFlow models on Google Cloud AI for real-time threat analysis and integrate with Chronicle for advanced threat intelligence.

Advantages of Cloud AI

- **Scalability**: Easily scale compute resources to handle increased data volumes.
- **Global Accessibility**: Enable remote security teams to collaborate and access AI tools.
- **Cost Efficiency**: Pay-as-you-go pricing models optimize costs for resource usage.

Summary

In this chapter, we have provided a hands-on guide for building AI models tailored to cybersecurity tasks. We've explored practical examples such as intrusion and malware detection, covered essential programming languages and libraries, and discussed optimization techniques. By following these steps and leveraging cloud-based resources, cybersecurity professionals can develop AI-powered systems that adapt to the evolving threat landscape, improving defense mechanisms and automating responses in real-time.

Chapter 9: Benefits of AI in Cybersecurity

Introduction

Cybersecurity is one of the most dynamic and high-stakes domains in technology. Organizations face increasing challenges from sophisticated cyber threats, limited resources, and the need to comply with evolving regulatory requirements. AI has emerged as a game-changing force, offering unparalleled capabilities to safeguard critical assets, streamline operations, and improve overall resilience. This chapter provides a comprehensive overview of how AI is reshaping the cybersecurity landscape, detailing its multifaceted benefits.

9.1 Proactive Threat Detection and Prevention

Traditional security measures often fall short in detecting novel or evolving threats, such as zero-day vulnerabilities, insider attacks, or advanced persistent threats (APTs). AI addresses these limitations by adopting a proactive approach:

- **Predictive Analysis**: AI models use predictive analytics to anticipate potential attack vectors based on historical data and trends. By leveraging techniques like predictive coding and heuristic analysis, AI can detect vulnerabilities before they are exploited.

- **Behavioral Analysis**: Unlike static security systems, AI continuously monitors user, device, and network behavior to detect deviations that may indicate malicious activities, such as unauthorized access or lateral movement within a network.

- **Integration with Threat Feeds**: AI seamlessly integrates with global threat intelligence feeds, allowing it to identify and counter emerging threats across industries and geographies.

Proactive threat detection enables organizations to stay ahead of attackers, reducing the risk of breaches and ensuring higher protection.

9.2 Reducing the Time to Detect and Respond to Incidents

The faster a threat is identified and mitigated, the less damage it can cause. AI plays a pivotal role in minimizing the time required to detect and respond to cyber incidents by:

- **AI-Powered SOCs**: Security Operations Centers (SOCs) equipped with AI systems can process vast amounts of data in real-time, identifying and prioritizing threats with remarkable speed.

- **Incident Correlation**: AI can correlate data from multiple sources, such as firewall logs, endpoint telemetry, and user activity, to provide a comprehensive picture of an incident. This contextual understanding accelerates decision-making.

- **Automated Remediation**: Once a threat is identified, AI can execute predefined actions, such as isolating affected devices, blocking malicious IP addresses, and initiating forensic analysis, significantly reducing manual intervention.

By drastically reducing response times, AI minimizes the potential impact of security breaches, helping organizations maintain business continuity.

9.3 Enhancing Security Operations and Automation

Security teams often face an overwhelming volume of alerts and routine tasks. AI transforms security operations by automating these processes, improving efficiency and effectiveness:

- **AI-Driven Workflows**: AI orchestrates workflows across various tools and platforms, ensuring seamless integration and faster resolution of security issues.

- **Dynamic Rule Updates**: AI systems can dynamically update firewall rules, intrusion prevention systems (IPS), and endpoint detection and response (EDR) configurations to address newly discovered threats.

- **Comprehensive Threat Hunting**: AI assists security analysts by automating threat hunting activities, allowing them to uncover hidden threats in large datasets without manual effort.

By enhancing automation, AI reduces the workload on human analysts and ensures that security operations remain agile and robust.

9.4 Improved Accuracy and Reduced False Positives

False positives are a significant challenge in cybersecurity, leading to wasted resources and analyst fatigue. AI enhances detection accuracy by:

- **Advanced Machine Learning Models**: AI algorithms learn from historical data to refine their ability to distinguish between legitimate activities and actual threats, improving detection accuracy over time.

- **Contextual Threat Analysis**: AI assesses the context of a potential threat, considering factors such as user behavior, device characteristics, and network conditions to determine its legitimacy.

- **Continuous Feedback Loops**: AI systems use feedback from security analysts to fine-tune their algorithms, ensuring ongoing improvements in performance.

With fewer false positives, security teams can focus their efforts on genuine threats, improving operational efficiency and reducing alert fatigue.

9.5 Cost-Effectiveness and Efficiency

Cybersecurity investments are often weighed against operational costs. AI offers a cost-effective solution by improving efficiency and reducing the resources required for effective security management:

- **Reduction in Manual Effort**: AI automates routine tasks like log analysis, vulnerability scanning, and incident reporting, allowing organizations to reallocate resources to strategic initiatives.

- **Lower Breach Costs**: Preventing breaches through proactive detection and mitigation reduces costs associated with recovery, legal fees, regulatory penalties, and reputational damage.

- **Optimized Resource Usage**: AI-driven security solutions can scale to meet the needs of growing organizations without proportional increases in staffing or infrastructure costs.

By optimizing resources and preventing costly incidents, AI delivers significant financial benefits while strengthening security.

9.6 Scalability and Flexibility

Cybersecurity solutions must be scalable and adaptable in today's dynamic business environments. AI provides the scalability and flexibility required to meet the demands of modern organizations:

- **Adaptability to Changing Threats**: AI continuously learns and evolves, enabling it to adapt to new attack vectors and techniques without requiring manual updates.

- **Cloud-Based AI Solutions**: Many AI-powered security solutions are cloud-based, offering flexible deployment options and the ability to protect distributed environments, including hybrid and multi-cloud infrastructures.

- **Support for IoT and Edge Security**: AI extends its capabilities to emerging technologies such as the Internet of Things (IoT) and edge computing, providing robust protection for these expanding ecosystems.

This scalability ensures that AI solutions can grow alongside organizations, maintaining consistent protection as needs evolve.

9.7 Empowering Security Analysts with AI Tools

Rather than replacing security analysts, AI amplifies their capabilities, enabling them to work more efficiently and effectively:

- **AI-Assisted Threat Analysis**: AI tools provide detailed insights into threat patterns, helping analysts understand complex attacks and craft effective responses.

- **Streamlined Investigation**: AI systems can generate comprehensive incident reports, including timelines, affected assets, and recommended actions, reducing the investigative burden on analysts.

- **Skill Augmentation**: AI equips analysts with advanced tools for tasks such as malware reverse engineering, vulnerability assessment, and penetration testing, enhancing their technical capabilities.

By empowering analysts with AI-driven insights and tools, organizations can improve the overall performance of their cybersecurity teams.

9.8 Leveraging AI for Cybersecurity Maturity Models

Cybersecurity maturity models (CMM) provide organizations with a framework for assessing and improving their security posture. AI plays a vital role in advancing maturity levels by:

- **Data-Driven Assessments**: AI collects and analyzes data from across the organization, providing a detailed view of current security practices and vulnerabilities.

- **Continuous Improvement Cycles**: AI helps organizations move toward higher maturity levels by identifying gaps and recommending actionable improvements.

- **Benchmarking and Metrics**: AI enables organizations to benchmark their cybersecurity practices against industry standards, ensuring alignment with best practices.

Integrating AI into CMM processes helps organizations achieve a more proactive, resilient, and adaptive security posture.

9.9 Benefits in Compliance and Regulatory Requirements

Meeting compliance and regulatory requirements is a critical aspect of cybersecurity. AI simplifies and enhances compliance efforts through:

- **Automated Monitoring and Reporting**: AI continuously monitors systems for compliance with regulatory frameworks and generates real-time compliance reports.

- **Enhanced Data Governance**: AI ensures proper handling of sensitive data, helping organizations adhere to data privacy regulations like GDPR and CCPA.

- **Audit Readiness**: AI systems can automatically collect and organize audit evidence, ensuring that organizations are prepared for inspections and assessments.

By streamlining compliance processes, AI reduces the administrative burden and ensures organizations remain compliant with evolving regulatory requirements.

Summary

The benefits of AI in cybersecurity are profound, transforming how organizations detect, prevent, and respond to threats. From proactive threat detection to improved operational efficiency and enhanced compliance, AI offers unmatched capabilities to fortify security infrastructures. As threats continue to evolve, the integration of AI will be critical for organizations aiming to protect their digital assets and ensure long-term resilience.

Chapter 10: AI for Threat Detection and Response

Introduction

AI has transformed cybersecurity by enabling faster, smarter, and more accurate detection and response to threats. This chapter explores how AI empowers organizations to stay ahead of evolving cyber threats, from zero-day exploits to insider threats, and discusses the future of AI in incident response.

10.1 Understanding Threat Detection with AI

AI in threat detection combines advanced machine learning (ML) algorithms, deep learning techniques, and large-scale data analysis to identify threats more effectively than traditional methods. Key capabilities include:

- **Pattern Recognition**: AI detects recurring malicious patterns, such as brute-force attacks, even in encrypted traffic.

- **Dynamic Learning**: Unlike static rule-based systems, AI adapts and learns from new threats.

- **Advanced Anomaly Detection**: AI uses baseline behavior models to identify deviations that may signal potential attacks.

- **Multi-Layered Security**: AI integrates data from multiple sources—endpoint logs, network activity, and user behavior—for a comprehensive analysis.

For example, AI can detect encrypted malicious payloads using behavioral analytics, which traditional signature-based detection might miss.

10.2 Types of Threats Detected by AI

AI can handle a broad spectrum of cyber threats, enhancing security defenses across the board.

Zero-Day Exploits

- **Definition**: Exploits targeting vulnerabilities that have not yet been disclosed or patched.

- **AI Role**: By examining software behavior and user interactions, AI algorithms predict zero-day vulnerabilities. Models trained on historical exploits can flag potential vulnerabilities in software.

- **Example**: AI tools like DeepExploit simulate penetration tests to uncover unpatched weaknesses before attackers do.

Ransomware Attacks

- **Definition**: Malicious software that encrypts files and demands ransom for decryption keys.

- **AI Role**: AI analyzes file activity for early signs of unauthorized encryption. Behavioral models can recognize and stop ransomware before it fully executes.

- **Example**: Tools like SentinelOne utilize deep learning to halt encryption attempts and isolate infected endpoints from the network.

Advanced Persistent Threats (APTs)

- **Definition**: Prolonged, targeted attacks designed to extract sensitive data from high-value targets.

- **AI Role**: AI analyzes slow and covert data extraction methods using UEBA to correlate activities across devices and time.

- **Example**: AI platforms like Darktrace monitor all network traffic, identifying patterns of lateral movement within a compromised environment.

Insider Threats

- **Definition**: Security risks originating from within the organization, whether intentional or accidental.

- **AI Role**: AI models analyze employee behavior, flagging deviations such as accessing unauthorized files or downloading large amounts of data at odd hours.

- **Example**: Using Natural Language Processing (NLP), AI analyzes communications for signs of disgruntled employee behavior or accidental sharing of sensitive information.

10.3 Real-Time Threat Response with AI

AI's ability to respond to threats in real-time is a cornerstone of modern cybersecurity. Its key functions include:

- **Behavior Monitoring**: AI systems continuously monitor network traffic and endpoint activity to identify threats in milliseconds.

- **Immediate Containment**: AI-powered systems can isolate infected devices, block malicious domains, and terminate suspicious processes without human intervention.

- **Dynamic Threat Intelligence Sharing**: AI systems update threat databases in real-time, sharing insights across security platforms globally.

- **Adaptive Threat Response**: AI learns from previous incidents, adapting to mitigate evolving threats more effectively.

For instance, AI-enabled firewalls can autonomously detect and block unauthorized access attempts, notifying security teams instantly.

10.4 AI for Automated Incident Handling

Automation significantly enhances the speed and accuracy of incident response. AI optimizes several processes:

Incident Classification

- **What It Does**: AI classifies incidents by type (e.g., phishing, malware) and severity, enabling prioritization.

- **Example**: An AI-powered Security Orchestration, Automation, and Response (SOAR) platform can differentiate between a critical server attack and a benign failed login attempt.

Root Cause Analysis

- **What It Does**: AI traces attack paths, identifies exploited vulnerabilities, and determines the entry point.

- **Example**: Graph-based AI tools visualize relationships between compromised systems, attackers, and data flows, pinpointing the source.

Automated Playbooks

- **What They Do**: AI executes predefined playbooks for specific incidents, such as blocking IP addresses or resetting compromised accounts.

- **Example**: In response to malware detection, an AI system can isolate affected endpoints and trigger alerts to IT teams.

10.5 AI and Human Collaboration in Threat Detection

Despite its advancements, AI cannot fully replace human judgment in cybersecurity. Collaboration between AI and human analysts leads to better outcomes.

- **Reducing Analyst Workload**: AI filters false positives, enabling analysts to focus on high-priority threats.

- **Providing Actionable Insights**: AI generates detailed reports on detected anomalies, helping analysts make informed decisions.

- **Interactive Learning**: Human feedback helps AI models improve their accuracy and relevance over time.

For instance, AI might flag unusual data downloads, but analysts determine whether it's a legitimate backup process or a malicious insider.

10.6 The Future of AI-Powered Incident Response

AI's role in cybersecurity will expand, driven by advancements in technology and the increasing complexity of cyber threats. Key trends include:

- **Proactive Threat Hunting**: AI will predict vulnerabilities and attack vectors before they are exploited.

- **Self-Healing Systems**: AI-enabled systems will automatically patch vulnerabilities and reconfigure themselves to avoid exploitation.

- **Quantum-AI Synergy**: As quantum computing advances, AI will leverage it for even faster threat analysis and cryptographic protections.

- **AI-Driven Cybersecurity Governance**: AI will assist organizations in maintaining compliance with evolving regulatory requirements.

10.7 Case Study: AI in Detecting and Mitigating Advanced Cyber Attacks

Background

A financial services firm experienced a targeted phishing campaign designed to compromise customer account credentials. Attackers aimed to gain unauthorized access to sensitive customer data and initiate fraudulent transactions.

AI Deployment

The organization deployed an AI-powered solution for proactive detection and response:

- **Phishing Email Detection**: NLP models flagged emails containing suspicious phrases and links to malicious websites.

- **User Behavior Analysis**: AI detected anomalies in account logins, such as unusual IP addresses or login times.

- **Automated Isolation**: Compromised accounts were immediately locked, preventing further access.

- **Threat Mitigation**: AI systems updated firewall rules to block access to attacker-controlled servers.

Results

- **Prevention**: No customer accounts were compromised due to immediate containment.

- **Enhanced Security**: Insights from the attack were used to strengthen email filtering and user authentication mechanisms.

Summary

AI revolutionizes threat detection and response by providing speed, precision, and scalability. From identifying zero-day exploits to automating incident handling, AI empowers organizations to tackle cyber threats effectively. By combining AI with human expertise, the future of cybersecurity promises enhanced resilience against an ever-changing threat landscape.

Chapter 11: Tools and Technologies in AI for Cybersecurity

Introduction

Cybersecurity is increasingly leveraging artificial intelligence (AI) to counter sophisticated threats. AI tools and technologies offer unparalleled capabilities to detect, respond to, and prevent cyber threats in real-time. This chapter dives deep into the landscape of AI tools, their unique features, and how to select the right solutions for diverse organizational needs.

11.1 Overview of AI Tools for Cybersecurity

AI tools for cybersecurity integrate machine learning (ML), natural language processing (NLP), and data analytics to strengthen cyber defenses. These tools perform various critical functions, including:

<u>Key Functions of AI in Cybersecurity</u>

- **Anomaly Detection**: Identifying unusual patterns that may indicate threats.

- **Behavioral Analytics**: Monitoring and analyzing user behavior to detect insider threats.

- **Incident Response**: Automating processes to mitigate risks quickly.

- **Threat Intelligence**: Collecting, analyzing, and acting on data about known and emerging threats.

The Importance of AI in Cybersecurity

- **Efficiency**: AI reduces reliance on manual processes, enhancing operational efficiency.

- **Speed**: Enables real-time detection and response to cyber incidents.

- **Scalability**: Handles vast datasets in large enterprises.

- **Adaptability**: Continuously learns and evolves to counter emerging threats.

11.2 AI-Powered Security Platforms

AI-powered platforms integrate multiple tools and technologies to offer comprehensive protection. They are essential for modern cybersecurity strategies.

Popular AI-Powered Platforms

1. **Darktrace**
   - **Overview**: Utilizes self-learning AI to detect threats without predefined rules.
   - **Key Features**:
     - Autonomous threat detection and response.
     - Behavioral analysis for anomaly detection.
   - **Real-World Application**: Effective in identifying ransomware attacks in real-time.
2. **CrowdStrike Falcon**
   - **Overview**: A cloud-native endpoint protection platform.
   - **Key Features**:
     - Threat intelligence for endpoint protection.
     - Lightweight agent for minimal system impact.
   - **Real-World Application**: Ideal for enterprises requiring endpoint security at scale.

3. **Cylance**
   o **Overview**: Focuses on proactive malware prevention.
   o **Key Features**:
     ▪ Signature-less detection.
     ▪ Low-resource AI models.
   o **Real-World Application**: Protects against malware in resource-constrained environments.

Additional Platforms: IBM QRadar and Splunk

- **IBM QRadar**:
  o Integrates SIEM and threat intelligence for real-time detection.
  o Provides advanced correlation of events across systems.
- **Splunk**:
  o Enables powerful log analysis and security automation.
  o Offers customizable dashboards for threat monitoring.

11.3 Security Automation Tools with AI Integration

Automation tools powered by AI are transforming incident response and security management.

Features of Security Automation Tools

- **Incident Triage**: Automatically prioritizes alerts to reduce noise.
- **Automated Playbooks**: Executes predefined workflows for common threats.
- **Integration**: Connects multiple systems for cohesive responses.

Top Tools for Security Automation

1. **Palo Alto Networks Cortex XSOAR**:
   o Combines orchestration with AI to automate workflows.
   o Integrates with hundreds of third-party tools.

2. **ServiceNow Security Operations**:
   - o Focuses on incident management and automated ticketing.
   - o Includes AI-driven risk scoring for alerts.

Benefits of Security Automation

- Reduces manual workload for security teams.
- Improves response times to contain threats faster.
- Enhances accuracy in handling repetitive tasks.

11.4 Open Source AI Tools in Cybersecurity

Open-source tools provide cost-effective and customizable solutions for organizations of all sizes.

Notable Open-Source AI Tools

1. **OpenAI**
   - o Provides powerful language models like GPT for security tasks.
   - o Applications include phishing detection and threat analysis.
2. **TensorFlow**
   - o Offers a robust framework for building custom AI models.
   - o Used for network intrusion detection and malware classification.

Other Open-Source Options

- **Keras**: Simplifies the development of AI models.
- **Scikit-Learn**: Ideal for data analysis and predictive modeling in cybersecurity.

Advantages of Open-Source Tools

- Cost-effective for organizations with tight budgets.
- Flexibility to customize tools based on specific needs.
- A large community of contributors ensures continuous improvement.

11.5 Choosing the Right AI Tools for Your Organization

Selecting the right AI tools requires a thorough understanding of organizational needs and the capabilities of available technologies.

Key Considerations

1. **Organizational Requirements**
   - Define the primary cybersecurity challenges (e.g., phishing, malware, insider threats).
2. **Tool Capabilities**
   - Assess the tool's ability to detect and respond to specific threats.
3. **Integration**
   - Ensure compatibility with existing infrastructure.
4. **Scalability**
   - Choose tools that can grow with organizational needs.

Steps for Effective Selection

- Conduct a gap analysis to identify current weaknesses.
- Evaluate multiple tools through trials or proof-of-concept implementations.
- Compare costs, features, and vendor support.

Common Pitfalls to Avoid

- Overinvesting in tools with redundant features.

- Neglecting user training and change management.
- Ignoring the importance of ongoing updates and maintenance.

11.6 Comparative Analysis of Top AI Cybersecurity Tools

Comparison Criteria

- **Core Capabilities**: Threat detection, response, and automation.
- **Ease of Deployment**: Cloud, on-premises, or hybrid.
- **Scalability**: Ability to handle large datasets and growing networks.
- **Integration**: Compatibility with existing security tools.
- **Cost-Effectiveness**: Balance of features versus pricing.

Sample Comparison Table

Feature	Darktrace	CrowdStrike	Cylance	QRadar	Splunk
Focus	Anomaly Detection	Endpoint Security	Malware Prevention	SIEM & Analysis	Orchestration
Deployment	Cloud/On-Prem	Cloud/Hybrid	Endpoint	On-Prem/Cloud	Cloud/On-Prem
Best Use Case	Ransomware	Enterprise EDR	SMB Malware	Log Analysis	Threat Automation

11.7 Case Study: The Best AI Tools for Enterprise Security

Background

A global financial services company faced escalating cyber threats, including phishing and ransomware attacks.

Challenges

- High volume of alerts overwhelmed the SOC.
- Advanced persistent threats (APTs) evaded traditional defenses.
- Manual incident response was slow, leading to prolonged recovery times.

Solutions Implemented

1. **Darktrace:**
   - Deployed for network-wide anomaly detection.
   - Identified and contained ransomware in its early stages.
2. **CrowdStrike Falcon:**
   - Provided endpoint protection with real-time threat intelligence.
   - Reduced malware incidents significantly.
3. **Splunk:**
   - Centralized log management and automated workflows for incident response.

Results

- Reduced alert fatigue by 70%.
- Incident response times improved by 60%.
- Achieved compliance with industry regulations through improved reporting.

Summary

AI tools and technologies are revolutionizing the cybersecurity industry. These tools offer robust defenses against evolving threats, from anomaly detection to automated incident response. Organizations can build resilient security frameworks to protect critical assets by carefully selecting and integrating AI solutions.

Chapter 12: Best Practices for Implementing AI in Cybersecurity

Introduction

Implementing AI in cybersecurity offers immense benefits, but it also presents unique challenges. To maximize the effectiveness of AI while minimizing risks, organizations must follow best practices that align AI solutions with their objectives, protect sensitive data, and foster a culture of innovation and ethical AI usage. This chapter outlines actionable steps and considerations for successfully implementing AI in cybersecurity.

12.1 Aligning AI Solutions with Business Objectives

AI implementation should address specific business challenges and goals rather than adopting technology for its own sake.

Steps to Align AI with Objectives

- **Define Objectives**:
    - Identify core cybersecurity challenges (e.g., ransomware prevention, anomaly detection).
    - Set measurable KPIs, such as reduced response time or improved detection accuracy.
- **Evaluate Use Cases**:
    - Prioritize use cases where AI offers the highest ROI, such as automating repetitive tasks or handling large datasets.
- **Integration Planning**:

o Assess how AI solutions will integrate with existing systems and workflows.
- **Stakeholder Collaboration**:
  o Involve cross-functional teams, including IT, compliance, and management, to ensure alignment with organizational priorities.

Example:

A financial institution might use AI to reduce fraud by implementing real-time anomaly detection models while ensuring compliance with regulatory standards.

12.2 Data Privacy and Security in AI Systems

AI relies heavily on data, making data privacy and security critical components of implementation.

Key Practices for Ensuring Privacy and Security

- **Data Minimization**:
  o Use only the necessary data for AI model training and analysis.
- **Anonymization**:
  o Mask or anonymize sensitive data to protect user identities.
- **Encryption**:
  o Ensure data is encrypted during storage and transmission.
- **Compliance Adherence**:
  o Align AI systems with data protection regulations like GDPR, HIPAA, or CCPA.
- **Secure Data Sources**:
  o Validate and secure data sources to prevent feeding compromised or malicious data into AI systems.

Challenges:

- Balancing the need for large datasets with privacy concerns.
- Protecting AI models from adversarial attacks targeting training data.

12.3 Balancing AI and Human Expertise

AI enhances cybersecurity capabilities but cannot replace human expertise. A balanced approach leverages both.

Strategies for Effective Collaboration

- **AI for Routine Tasks**:
  o Use AI to automate repetitive tasks such as log analysis or phishing email identification.
- **Humans for Strategic Oversight**:
  o Let security analysts focus on strategic decisions and complex incidents.
- **Training Security Teams**:
  o Educate teams on how to interpret AI outputs and make informed decisions.
- **Feedback Loops**:
  o Enable humans to provide feedback to improve AI model performance over time.

Example:

In a SOC, AI tools flag potential threats while analysts review and validate the findings to determine the appropriate response.

12.4 Regular Model Training and Maintenance

AI models must adapt to evolving threat landscapes to remain effective.

Best Practices for Model Training

- **Continuous Learning**:
  - o Update models with the latest threat intelligence to enhance detection accuracy.
- **Dataset Validation**:
  - o Ensure training datasets are accurate, diverse, and free of bias.
- **Performance Monitoring**:
  - o Track model performance metrics such as precision, recall, and F1 score.
- **Periodic Retraining**:
  - o Retrain models regularly to address emerging threats and maintain relevance.

Challenges:

- Managing computational resources for frequent retraining.
- Identifying and mitigating data drift in dynamic environments.

12.5 Ethical AI in Cybersecurity

AI-driven cybersecurity must adhere to ethical guidelines to ensure fairness, transparency, and accountability.

Principles of Ethical AI

- **Transparency**:
  - o Ensure stakeholders understand how AI models make decisions.
- **Accountability**:
  - o Assign responsibility for AI outcomes to specific teams or individuals.
- **Bias Mitigation**:

o Regularly audit AI models for potential biases in decision-making.
- **Human Oversight:**
  o Keep humans in the loop for critical decisions to prevent unintended consequences.

Real-World Implications:

Unethical AI use in cybersecurity, such as surveillance without consent, can damage organizational reputation and lead to legal repercussions.

12.6 Reducing AI-Driven False Positives

High false-positive rates can overwhelm security teams and reduce trust in AI systems.

Approaches to Minimize False Positives

- **Model Tuning:**
  o Optimize thresholds and parameters for more accurate predictions.
- **Advanced Algorithms:**
  o Use ensemble methods or deep learning for better threat detection.
- **Data Quality:**
  o Ensure input data is accurate and relevant to reduce noise.
- **Alert Prioritization:**
  o Rank alerts based on risk severity to focus on high-impact threats.

Benefits:

- Reduces alert fatigue among security teams.
- Enhances trust in AI-driven systems.

12.7 Continuous Monitoring and Improvement of AI Models

AI systems require ongoing evaluation and refinement to ensure sustained effectiveness.

Monitoring Best Practices

- **Real-Time Performance Tracking:**
    o Use dashboards to monitor model metrics and identify anomalies.
- **Feedback Mechanisms:**
    o Incorporate feedback from analysts and users to improve AI systems.
- **Threat Landscape Updates:**
    o Regularly update AI tools with the latest threat intelligence.
- **Error Analysis:**
    o Investigate false positives and negatives to enhance accuracy.

12.8 Conducting Risk Assessments for AI-Powered Security Tools

Risk assessments help identify potential vulnerabilities and ensure robust AI implementations.

Steps in AI Risk Assessment

1. **Threat Identification:**
    o Evaluate risks such as adversarial attacks or model poisoning.
2. **Impact Analysis:**
    o Assess the potential damage of AI failures or breaches.
3. **Mitigation Planning:**
    o Develop strategies to address identified risks.

4. **Regular Audits**:
    o Conduct periodic reviews to identify and mitigate emerging risks.

Tools for Risk Assessments

- NIST Cybersecurity Framework.
- AI-specific risk analysis tools such as LIME and SHAP.

12.9 Creating an AI-Enabled Cybersecurity Culture

Building a culture that embraces AI is essential for successful adoption.

Key Elements of an AI-Enabled Culture

- **Leadership Support**:
    o Ensure leaders champion AI initiatives.
- **Employee Training**:
    o Train employees to understand and use AI tools effectively.
- **Innovation Encouragement**:
    o Foster an environment that supports experimentation with AI.
- **Cross-Functional Collaboration**:
    o Promote collaboration between IT, cybersecurity, and data science teams.

Benefits of an AI-Driven Culture

- Increased trust and confidence in AI implementations.
- Higher adoption rates across the organization.
- Enhanced adaptability to future cybersecurity challenges.

Summary

Implementing AI in cybersecurity is a strategic necessity in the modern threat landscape. By following best practices—ranging from aligning AI with business objectives to fostering an AI-enabled culture— organizations can maximize the benefits of AI while mitigating associated risks. With continuous monitoring, ethical considerations, and collaboration between AI and human expertise, AI can serve as a cornerstone of resilient and proactive cybersecurity strategies.

Chapter 13: The Dark Side of AI in Cybersecurity

Introduction

Artificial Intelligence has become a double-edged sword in cybersecurity. While its potential for enhancing defenses is undeniable, it is also being weaponized by malicious actors. This chapter delves into how AI is leveraged for sophisticated cyberattacks, the ethical dilemmas it presents, and strategies to counter these evolving threats.

13.1 The Rise of AI-Driven Cyber Attacks

AI-driven cyberattacks represent a significant shift in the threat landscape. These attacks are characterized by their automation, scalability, and ability to adapt in real-time. Traditional attacks often rely on human intervention, which limits their speed and scale. However, AI enables cybercriminals to automate complex tasks, such as scanning for vulnerabilities or generating malicious code, with unparalleled efficiency.

The adaptability of AI-driven attacks is particularly concerning. These systems can learn from failed attempts, modify their approaches, and exploit weaknesses in defenses more effectively than ever before. For example, AI-powered tools can analyze network traffic to identify patterns and vulnerabilities, allowing attackers to execute targeted exploits with precision. This rise in sophistication has made detecting and mitigating such threats an increasingly challenging task.

Emerging trends in AI-driven cyberattacks include the use of generative AI to create fake identities, synthetic media, and deepfake content. These advancements make it easier for attackers to deceive victims and bypass traditional verification methods, further complicating the defensive measures required to counter these threats.

13.2 AI in Phishing and Social Engineering

AI has transformed phishing and social engineering into highly targeted and effective methods of attack. Traditional phishing campaigns often involve generic emails sent to a wide audience, relying on chance to succeed. In contrast, AI enables the creation of personalized phishing messages that are more convincing and difficult to detect.

Deepfake technology is a prime example of AI's impact on social engineering. With AI-generated audio and video, attackers can impersonate individuals with astonishing accuracy. These deepfakes can be used to manipulate victims into divulging sensitive information or authorizing fraudulent transactions. Similarly, AI-driven chatbots have been employed in real-time interactions to extract confidential data from unsuspecting users.

The scale and success of these AI-powered techniques have grown significantly, as they can analyze social media profiles, communication habits, and other data sources to craft messages that resonate with individual targets. This level of personalization makes detecting phishing attempts increasingly difficult for both individuals and automated systems.

13.3 AI-Powered Malware and Ransomware

AI is enhancing traditional malware and giving rise to a new generation of adaptive and evasive threats. AI-powered malware can dynamically modify its code to avoid detection by security systems. This polymorphic behavior makes traditional signature-based detection methods obsolete, forcing defenders to rely on more advanced behavioral analysis.

Ransomware has also benefited from AI advancements. Modern ransomware uses AI algorithms to optimize encryption processes, ensuring that files are locked quickly and effectively. Additionally, ransomware campaigns have become more targeted, using AI to identify high-value targets and tailor ransom demands accordingly. For example, attackers can analyze an organization's financial records and operational data to set a ransom amount that is more likely to be paid.

AI-powered malware is also capable of executing context-aware attacks. By analyzing the environment it operates in, such as the operating system and security configurations, the malware can adjust its behavior to maximize impact while minimizing the likelihood of detection.

13.4 Adversarial AI: Attacking AI Models

Adversarial AI is a growing concern in cybersecurity, as it targets the very systems designed to protect against threats. By exploiting vulnerabilities in AI models, attackers can undermine their effectiveness and even use them against the organizations that deploy them. One common tactic is evasion attacks, where attackers manipulate inputs to fool AI systems into misclassifying malicious activities as benign.

Model poisoning is another significant threat involving the introduction of malicious data during the training process. This type of attack compromises the integrity of the AI model, causing it to behave unpredictably or inaccurately. Additionally, attackers often reverse-engineer AI models to identify weaknesses that can be exploited to bypass defenses.

These adversarial techniques highlight the need for robust and secure AI model development practices. Without proper safeguards, AI-powered systems can become liabilities rather than assets.

13.5 Ethical Dilemmas in AI-Powered Cybersecurity

The use of AI in cybersecurity raises numerous ethical questions. One of the most pressing concerns is the potential for bias in AI models. Since AI systems learn from historical data, they can inherit and amplify biases present in the data. This can lead to unfair outcomes, such as disproportionately targeting certain groups or overlooking specific types of threats.

Another ethical dilemma is the dual-use nature of AI technologies. Tools developed for legitimate purposes, such as network monitoring or threat detection, can be repurposed by cybercriminals to carry out attacks. This raises questions about the responsibility of developers and organizations in ensuring that their AI systems are not misused.

Autonomous decision-making by AI systems also poses ethical challenges. Delegating critical cybersecurity decisions to machines can lead to unintended consequences, particularly in scenarios where human oversight is absent. Ensuring accountability and transparency in AI operations is essential to addressing these ethical concerns.

13.6 Addressing the Vulnerabilities of AI in Cyber Defense

While AI has significantly enhanced cyber defenses, it is not without its vulnerabilities. Overreliance on AI can create blind spots, as these systems may fail to recognize emerging threats or adapt to novel attack techniques. Additionally, AI models are heavily dependent on the quality and quantity of data used for training. Poorly curated data can lead to inaccurate predictions and missed threats.

Another critical vulnerability lies in the resource-intensive nature of AI systems. Attackers can exploit this by launching denial-of-service attacks targeting the computational infrastructure supporting AI defenses. This can cripple an organization's ability to respond to threats effectively.

Mitigating these vulnerabilities requires a layered approach to cybersecurity. Combining AI with traditional security measures, regularly updating models, and ensuring robust data management practices are crucial for maintaining the effectiveness of AI-powered defenses.

13.7 The Impact of AI on Privacy and Surveillance

AI's capabilities for analyzing vast amounts of data have significant implications for privacy and surveillance. Organizations and governments increasingly rely on AI to monitor user behavior, detect anomalies, and enforce compliance. While these applications improve security, they also raise concerns about overreach and potential misuse.

Mass surveillance enabled by AI can infringe on individual rights, particularly when data is collected without consent. Profiling and tracking technologies powered by AI can create detailed digital footprints, often without the user's knowledge. This level of monitoring poses a threat to personal privacy and can lead to abuse if not properly regulated.

Balancing the benefits of AI-driven surveillance with the need for privacy requires strict regulatory frameworks and ethical guidelines. Techniques such as federated learning, which allows AI models to train on decentralized data, can help protect privacy while maintaining effectiveness.

13.8 Mitigating AI-Driven Risks and Threats

Organizations must adopt a proactive and comprehensive approach to counter the risks associated with AI in cybersecurity. One critical strategy is leveraging AI itself to combat AI-driven threats. AI can identify and predict emerging attack vectors by gathering and analyzing threat intelligence.

Adversarial testing is another essential practice where AI systems are tested against potential attack scenarios to identify weaknesses. This process helps organizations build more resilient models capable of withstanding adversarial tactics. Human-AI collaboration also plays a crucial role, combining AI's analytical power with cybersecurity professionals' intuition and expertise.

Education and awareness are equally important. Training employees to recognize AI-driven threats, such as deepfakes and sophisticated phishing attempts, empowers them to act as the first line of defense. Additionally, adhering to regulatory requirements and ethical standards ensures that AI implementations are both effective and responsible.

Summary

The dark side of AI in cybersecurity highlights the dual-use nature of this technology. While it has revolutionized threat detection and response, it has also equipped cybercriminals with powerful tools for exploitation. Understanding and addressing these challenges is vital for building resilient and ethical cybersecurity strategies. By fostering collaboration between humans and AI, organizations can harness the potential of AI while mitigating its risks.

Chapter 14: The Future of AI in Cybersecurity

Introduction

The intersection of artificial intelligence (AI) and cybersecurity continues to evolve, offering new opportunities and challenges. This chapter explores the emerging trends, transformative effects, and potential implications of AI in shaping the cybersecurity landscape.

14.1 Emerging Trends in AI and Cybersecurity

AI is increasingly deployed to address complex security challenges as the digital world becomes more interconnected. Several key trends are reshaping the future of cybersecurity:

AI for Quantum Computing and Cyber Defense

Quantum computing, while promising revolutionary computational power, also introduces significant risks to cryptography, a cornerstone of cybersecurity. AI plays a critical role in developing quantum-resistant algorithms and monitoring quantum-based threats. AI-driven analytics can also predict vulnerabilities in quantum systems, ensuring preparedness against quantum-enabled attacks.

AI in Cloud Security and IoT

The proliferation of cloud computing and Internet of Things (IoT) devices has expanded the attack surface for cyber threats. AI enhances cloud security by analyzing massive data sets for anomalous behavior, enforcing compliance standards, and automating incident responses. In

IoT, AI helps secure connected devices by monitoring device activity, identifying unauthorized access, and managing firmware vulnerabilities.

AI-Driven Cybersecurity for Autonomous Systems

The rise of autonomous systems, such as self-driving cars and drones, presents unique security challenges. AI is essential for safeguarding these systems, ensuring they can identify and respond to cyber threats in real-time. By leveraging AI, autonomous systems can detect anomalies, prevent malicious interference, and maintain operational integrity.

14.2 The Role of AI in Cybersecurity Workforce Transformation

AI is not only changing how cybersecurity tasks are performed but also redefining the workforce's role. By automating repetitive tasks such as log analysis and threat detection, AI allows security professionals to focus on more strategic activities, such as risk management and incident response planning.

Moreover, AI is fostering the need for upskilled professionals who can develop, manage, and interpret AI-driven tools. Training programs in AI for cybersecurity are becoming integral to workforce development, ensuring that professionals can work alongside AI systems effectively.

Collaborative intelligence, where humans and AI systems work in tandem, will define the future workforce. AI provides rapid data analysis and pattern recognition, while human experts bring contextual understanding and ethical judgment, creating a synergy that enhances cybersecurity operations.

14.3 Potential Ethical, Legal, and Social Implications of AI in Cybersecurity

The integration of AI into cybersecurity raises significant ethical, legal, and social concerns. One key issue is the transparency of AI algorithms. Decision-making processes in AI systems often lack interpretability, making it difficult to hold entities accountable for errors or biases.

Privacy is another major concern. AI-driven monitoring systems analyze vast amounts of personal data, which can lead to invasive surveillance practices if not regulated appropriately. Balancing security and privacy will require robust policies and ethical frameworks.

The legal implications of AI in cybersecurity are also evolving. Questions about liability in AI-driven decisions, particularly in automated incident responses, remain unresolved. Organizations must navigate these uncertainties while ensuring compliance with existing regulations.

14.4 The Evolution of AI Technologies and Their Impact on Security

AI technologies are advancing rapidly, with innovations such as reinforcement learning, generative AI, and neural networks significantly impacting cybersecurity. These technologies enable more sophisticated threat detection, predictive analytics, and automated responses.

For example, generative AI can create synthetic data sets to train cybersecurity models, improving their accuracy and resilience. Neural networks can analyze complex relationships in data, enabling early detection of multi-vector attacks. As these technologies evolve, their integration into cybersecurity strategies will become more seamless and impactful.

The increasing adoption of edge AI, where AI computations are performed locally on devices rather than centralized servers, is also transforming security. Edge AI reduces latency, enhances privacy, and enables faster responses to threats in environments such as IoT networks.

14.5 AI in the Era of Increasing Cyber Threats

The frequency and sophistication of cyber threats are growing, driven by advancements in attack techniques and the expanding digital landscape.

AI is becoming a critical tool in countering these threats, offering real-time analysis, adaptive responses, and predictive capabilities.

AI-powered systems can process massive volumes of data to identify patterns indicative of cyberattacks. Machine learning models can adapt to new threats by continuously learning from evolving attack vectors. These capabilities enable organizations to stay ahead of adversaries and mitigate risks effectively.

However, as AI strengthens defenses, attackers are also leveraging AI to enhance their tactics. AI-generated malware, deepfake phishing campaigns, and adversarial AI attacks are becoming increasingly common. This arms race between attackers and defenders underscores the need for constant innovation in AI-driven cybersecurity.

14.6 Advancements in AI-Powered Cyber Defense for Future Threats

AI continues to revolutionize cyber defense strategies, enabling proactive approaches to emerging threats. Future advancements include the integration of AI with blockchain technology for enhanced data security and the use of AI-driven deception techniques to mislead attackers.

The development of federated learning, where AI models are trained across decentralized data sources without sharing raw data, promises to improve collaboration across organizations while maintaining privacy. This approach is particularly useful in industries where data sharing is restricted, such as healthcare and finance.

AI's role in automated threat intelligence sharing is also expanding. By standardizing and disseminating threat intelligence across sectors, AI enables organizations to respond more effectively to global threats.

14.7 AI as a Game-Changer in Cybersecurity Operations

AI is fundamentally transforming how cybersecurity operations are conducted. Its ability to automate and optimize processes reduces response times, enhances accuracy, and lowers operational costs. For example, Security Operations Centers (SOCs) increasingly rely on AI to filter alerts, prioritize incidents, and provide actionable insights.

In addition to operational improvements, AI is driving innovation in security architecture. AI-powered predictive analytics enable organizations to identify vulnerabilities before they are exploited. Adaptive security frameworks, supported by AI, can dynamically adjust defenses based on real-time threat assessments.

The integration of AI into cybersecurity operations is not without challenges, including the risk of overreliance and the need for skilled personnel. However, the benefits far outweigh these concerns, making AI a game-changer in achieving robust and efficient cybersecurity.

Summary

The future of AI in cybersecurity is both promising and complex. Emerging trends such as quantum computing, IoT security, and autonomous systems will redefine the threat landscape, while advancements in AI technologies will enhance defense mechanisms. Ethical considerations, workforce transformation, and evolving operational strategies will shape how AI is deployed in cybersecurity. By embracing these changes and addressing the challenges, organizations can harness AI's potential to create a safer digital environment.

Chapter 15: Solutions and Recommendations

Introduction

AI's role in cybersecurity is becoming indispensable as organizations face increasingly sophisticated and pervasive threats. This chapter focuses on how organizations can implement AI-driven solutions to enhance their cybersecurity posture. It provides practical recommendations, strategic advice, and case studies that guide businesses in leveraging AI to build robust, resilient security frameworks.

15.1 Building an AI-Driven Security Strategy

An AI-driven security strategy begins with understanding the organization's specific cybersecurity needs and the types of threats it faces. This requires collaboration across IT, security, and risk management departments to ensure alignment between AI solutions and business goals. AI should not be seen as a standalone tool but as an integral part of a broader security strategy that encompasses prevention, detection, response, and recovery.

The first step in building a strategy is assessing the organization's security landscape. This includes evaluating existing security measures such as firewalls, intrusion detection systems, and threat intelligence platforms. From there, organizations can identify gaps in their security posture where AI can play a pivotal role. For instance, if the organization struggles with detecting advanced persistent threats (APTs) or insider threats, AI technologies like machine learning (ML) and behavioral analytics can be integrated into the network monitoring systems to spot unusual activity.

AI's role in automation is also critical to an effective strategy. For example, AI can automate repetitive tasks like log analysis, freeing up security professionals to focus on more complex challenges. Moreover, AI-driven tools can help prioritize alerts based on severity, reducing the burden of false positives. In designing this strategy, organizations should establish clear key performance indicators (KPIs) to track the success of AI integration, including improved threat detection rates, reduced response times, and the ability to stop attacks before they cause damage.

Finally, the AI-driven security strategy should incorporate feedback mechanisms to continuously improve over time. As new threats emerge and AI models are refined, the strategy should evolve to accommodate these changes, ensuring that AI remains effective and aligned with organizational objectives.

15.2 Integrating AI into Existing Cybersecurity Frameworks

Integrating AI into an existing cybersecurity framework is a multi-step process that requires a thoughtful approach to technology, people, and processes. The first consideration is the compatibility of AI tools with the organization's current IT and security infrastructure. Many AI solutions have APIs that can easily integrate with security platforms such as Security Information and Event Management (SIEM) systems, endpoint protection tools, and firewalls. It's essential to assess which components of the infrastructure will benefit the most from AI, ensuring that resources are allocated efficiently.

One of the primary integration challenges is data. AI models require large datasets to be trained and refined; this data needs to be clean, well-organized, and accessible. Organizations must implement robust data collection processes that aggregate data from different sources, such as network traffic, user behavior, and threat intelligence feeds. Integrating AI into cybersecurity systems may also require the adoption of new data storage solutions or platforms to ensure that the vast amounts of data needed for AI analysis can be efficiently stored and processed.

Another critical factor in integration is organizational readiness. The cybersecurity team must be adequately trained in how to use AI-driven tools and interpret the results generated by these systems. Change management processes should be in place to guide teams through the integration, ensuring minimal disruption. This may include conducting workshops, providing hands-on training, and ensuring that AI tools are intuitive and user-friendly to reduce the learning curve for cybersecurity professionals.

Lastly, businesses should prioritize scalability when integrating AI. As the organization's security needs grow, the AI tools should be able to scale without compromising performance. Cloud-based AI solutions offer scalability advantages and are often easier to integrate into existing frameworks compared to on-premise solutions.

15.3 Addressing AI Vulnerabilities in Cybersecurity

AI-powered cybersecurity systems are not immune to vulnerabilities. While AI offers advanced threat detection capabilities, it also introduces new risks that need to be carefully managed. One of the most significant concerns is adversarial attacks, where cybercriminals manipulate AI models by feeding them specially crafted inputs. For example, an attacker could alter the data fed into a machine learning model to deceive it into misclassifying malicious activity as benign, thus evading detection.

Organizations should implement robust security measures for their AI systems to mitigate these risks. This includes conducting adversarial testing and training AI models with diverse, high-quality data covering various attack scenarios. Adversarial machine learning techniques can also be used to make AI models more resistant to manipulation.

Another area of concern is the transparency and interpretability of AI models. Many machine learning algorithms, especially deep learning models, function as "black boxes," meaning it can be difficult to understand how they make decisions. This lack of transparency raises concerns about accountability, particularly in security-sensitive environments where decisions made by AI can have serious consequences.

To address this, organizations can employ explainable AI (XAI) techniques. XAI aims to make the decision-making process of AI models more understandable to humans by providing insights into the model's inner workings. This increases trust in AI systems and helps security professionals intervene when AI makes an incorrect decision or flags a false positive.

Additionally, the cybersecurity team should regularly audit AI models to identify biases or weaknesses that could be exploited. The use of continuous model evaluation, combined with manual oversight, ensures that AI tools are not just implemented but are also functioning as intended and evolving alongside new threats.

15.4 Leveraging AI for Resilience Against Future Cyber Attacks

AI offers organizations the opportunity to build resilience against future cyberattacks through proactive threat detection and continuous improvement. One of the key advantages of AI in cybersecurity is its ability to detect new, previously unknown threats by analyzing patterns in vast amounts of data. For instance, AI can learn what normal network traffic looks like and immediately identify anomalies that may indicate a potential attack.

Predictive analytics powered by AI can also play a crucial role in identifying vulnerabilities before attackers exploit them. By analyzing historical attack data, threat intelligence, and behavioral patterns, AI systems can predict where future attacks might occur, allowing organizations to take preventative measures.

Automating incident response is another critical component of leveraging AI for resilience. Once a threat is detected, AI can take immediate action, such as isolating a compromised device from the network, blocking malicious IP addresses, or terminating suspicious processes. This rapid response minimizes the damage caused by attacks and helps the organization recover more quickly.

For long-term resilience, organizations can use AI-driven simulations and threat intelligence to test their security infrastructure. AI can simulate a wide range of attack scenarios, from DDoS attacks to advanced persistent threats, enabling organizations to evaluate their response strategies and identify weaknesses before a real attack occurs.

15.5 Case Studies: Successful AI Cybersecurity Implementations

Many organizations have successfully implemented AI-driven cybersecurity solutions, demonstrating the potential of AI to revolutionize cybersecurity operations.

Darktrace, for example, is widely recognized for its AI-powered cybersecurity platform. Using machine learning algorithms, Darktrace's system continuously analyzes network traffic to detect unusual patterns that could indicate a cyberattack. The system uses unsupervised learning, meaning it doesn't rely on predefined rules or attack signatures. This allows it to adapt to new, previously unseen threats in real-time. Darktrace's self-learning AI model can autonomously respond to threats by taking actions such as shutting down malicious activity or quarantining affected systems, reducing the need for human intervention.

CrowdStrike, another prominent player, uses AI to enhance endpoint protection. Its Falcon platform leverages machine learning algorithms to detect and respond to threats based on behavioral patterns. The AI system can distinguish between normal and abnormal behavior, enabling it to identify suspicious activities like lateral movement within a network or attempts to exfiltrate sensitive data. Falcon's AI-driven capabilities significantly improve threat detection while reducing false positives, allowing security teams to focus on real threats.

Cylance employs AI to prevent malware and ransomware attacks before they execute. By analyzing file behaviors, Cylance's AI system can predict which files are likely to be malicious and block them before they cause harm. The system operates without relying on traditional signature-based detection, making it highly effective against zero-day exploits and polymorphic malware.

These case studies illustrate how AI is transforming cybersecurity operations by enabling more effective threat detection, faster response times, and enhanced protection across multiple layers of an organization's IT infrastructure.

15.6 How to Future-Proof Your Cybersecurity Operations with AI

The rapidly evolving threat landscape requires that organizations continuously adapt their cybersecurity practices. To future-proof cybersecurity operations, businesses must embrace a forward-thinking approach to AI adoption.

One key aspect of future-proofing is adopting adaptive AI technologies that can learn and evolve as new threats emerge. Machine learning algorithms, for example, should be regularly retrained on new data to ensure they can identify novel attack patterns. This continuous learning process helps organizations stay one step ahead of cybercriminals.

Organizations should also invest in scalable AI solutions that can grow with their needs. As the volume of data increases and cyber threats become more complex, scalable solutions ensure that AI systems can handle the expanded workload without compromising performance.

Collaboration with other emerging technologies is another crucial factor in future-proofing cybersecurity. Integrating AI with blockchain, for example, can help prevent fraud and ensure data integrity. Similarly, AI-powered systems can be paired with quantum computing in the future to address more complex cybersecurity challenges that today's technologies cannot handle.

Lastly, to maintain a competitive edge, organizations must stay up to date with AI advancements by fostering a culture of innovation. This includes investing in research and development, attending industry conferences, and engaging with thought leaders to explore the latest AI-driven cybersecurity solutions.

15.7 Developing a Roadmap for AI-Driven Security Innovation

Developing a roadmap for AI-driven security innovation is essential for organizations looking to leverage AI as part of their long-term security strategy. The roadmap should align with the organization's overall cybersecurity and business objectives while also addressing specific security challenges.

The first step is to thoroughly assess the organization's current security posture, identifying vulnerabilities, gaps, and areas where AI can add value. Once these areas have been identified, organizations should define clear goals for AI adoption, such as improving threat detection accuracy, automating incident response, or enhancing data protection.

The roadmap should also outline the specific AI technologies and tools that will be implemented, along with an estimated timeline for their deployment. This phased approach allows for the gradual integration and testing of AI systems, ensuring minimal disruption and optimizing the adoption process.

A key component of the roadmap is establishing performance metrics to evaluate the effectiveness of AI systems. These metrics should be tied to specific security outcomes, such as reduced response time or increased detection of advanced threats.

Finally, the roadmap should include provisions for continuous improvement. As AI technologies evolve and new threats emerge, the organization should regularly review and refine its AI strategy to ensure that it remains effective and aligned with changing cybersecurity challenges.

Summary

AI-driven cybersecurity solutions are critical for organizations seeking to defend against increasingly sophisticated threats. However, successfully implementing AI in cybersecurity requires careful planning, integration, and ongoing refinement. By developing a comprehensive AI-driven security strategy, integrating AI with existing systems, and addressing potential vulnerabilities, organizations can build a robust and resilient defense against cyberattacks. As AI continues to evolve, businesses must stay agile, adapting their strategies and technologies to maintain a proactive defense against future threats. Through continuous innovation and adaptation, AI can serve as a powerful ally in the ongoing battle against cybercrime.

Chapter 16: Career in AI and Cybersecurity

Introduction

The convergence of artificial intelligence (AI) and cybersecurity is reshaping the industry, offering exciting career prospects for professionals who can blend these two domains. As cyber threats become more complex and AI-driven technologies gain ground, cybersecurity professionals who understand how to leverage AI for defense will be in high demand. This chapter explores the growing need for AI-driven cybersecurity experts, the essential skills for success, career paths in the field, and how AI will influence job roles in cybersecurity.

16.1 Growing Demand for AI in Cybersecurity Professionals

The demand for AI in cybersecurity is increasing rapidly, driven by the rise in cyber threats and the growing complexity of digital infrastructures. Organizations across various industries, from financial services to healthcare, are realizing the need for advanced technologies like AI to protect sensitive data and prevent security breaches. AI's ability to process large datasets, identify patterns, and predict potential attacks in real-time is revolutionizing how cybersecurity functions are carried out. This has led to a surge in demand for cybersecurity professionals with specialized knowledge in AI.

Cybercriminals continuously evolve their tactics, leveraging AI to carry out more sophisticated attacks, such as automated phishing, malware creation, and network intrusions. To counter these emerging threats, companies need AI-powered tools that can analyze vast amounts of data, detect anomalies, and respond to threats more quickly than traditional security measures allow. The intersection of AI and cybersecurity offers a fertile ground for growth, creating a wealth of opportunities for professionals who are proficient in both fields. In fact, the shortage of skilled cybersecurity professionals is expected to widen, with AI expertise becoming a key differentiator for those entering the workforce.

According to industry reports, the number of AI-related job postings in cybersecurity is projected to grow exponentially in the coming years, outpacing demand for traditional cybersecurity roles. This represents a unique opportunity for professionals looking to future-proof their careers by developing expertise in AI-driven security technologies.

16.2 Key Skills for a Career in AI-Driven Cybersecurity

Professionals entering the AI and cybersecurity space must equip themselves with a diverse skill set that spans both technical and strategic areas. The following competencies are vital for anyone looking to build a successful career in AI-driven cybersecurity:

1. Machine Learning and Deep Learning

Machine learning (ML) and deep learning (DL) are at the heart of AI applications in cybersecurity. Professionals must understand how algorithms learn from data to detect anomalies and predict future cyber threats. Proficiency in training ML models to recognize suspicious patterns in network traffic, user behavior, or system activity is essential. Knowledge of supervised, unsupervised, and reinforcement learning is crucial, as these techniques help build the models that power AI-driven cybersecurity solutions.

Deep learning, which involves neural networks with multiple layers, is particularly useful in tasks such as image recognition (e.g., identifying malware) and natural language processing (e.g., detecting phishing emails). Understanding how to implement and fine-tune deep learning models is becoming increasingly important for those working in AI-based security systems.

2. Data Science and Analytics

AI thrives on data, and the ability to analyze and interpret large datasets is essential. Professionals in AI-driven cybersecurity must be adept at data science techniques, including data preprocessing, statistical modeling, and data visualization. This skill set enables cybersecurity experts to analyze network traffic, identify anomalies, and draw actionable insights from security data. A solid understanding of data processing frameworks such as Hadoop or Spark can be beneficial when working with big data in cybersecurity applications.

Being able to distill insights from vast amounts of data can also help in predictive analytics, allowing professionals to anticipate potential security threats before they occur. The ability to transform raw data into actionable intelligence is one of the cornerstones of AI-driven security.

3. Cybersecurity Fundamentals

While AI is a powerful tool in cybersecurity, a strong grasp of traditional security principles remains essential. Professionals must understand core cybersecurity concepts such as network security, firewalls, encryption, and identity management. They should also be familiar with common attack vectors, including Distributed Denial of Service (DDoS), ransomware, insider threats, and phishing.

AI models are built on these traditional principles, enhancing them with automation, speed, and predictive capabilities. Professionals will struggle to design and implement effective AI solutions without understanding the fundamentals of how cybersecurity defenses work. Knowledge of compliance standards and regulations, such as GDPR and NIST, is also critical when working with sensitive data.

4. Programming and Scripting Languages

Programming is an indispensable skill for anyone working in AI and cybersecurity. Python, R, Java, and C++ are widely used for building machine learning models and AI-driven security tools. Python, in particular, is favored for its ease of use and the vast range of machine learning libraries (e.g., TensorFlow, Keras, and scikit-learn) available for developing AI models.

Scripting languages such as Bash, PowerShell, or JavaScript can help automate vulnerability scanning, incident response, and log management tasks. These languages enable cybersecurity professionals to create custom solutions that fit specific organizational needs, enhancing the overall security posture.

5. Threat Intelligence and Risk Assessment

AI-based cybersecurity tools are often designed to process and analyze threat intelligence in real-time, providing deeper insights into the threat landscape. Professionals should be skilled in working with threat intelligence platforms and feeds, and understanding how AI can be used to correlate and analyze data across various sources (e.g., dark web monitoring, honeypots, and vulnerability databases).

Risk assessment is another key area where AI can play a vital role. Professionals need to assess the risks posed by specific threats, evaluate the effectiveness of security measures, and develop AI models that can automatically adjust defense mechanisms based on evolving threat intelligence.

6. Cloud Computing and Virtualization

Cloud environments are increasingly becoming targets for cyberattacks, and many AI-driven security solutions are deployed in the cloud. As such, professionals should have expertise in cloud security practices and technologies, particularly in relation to AI. Knowledge of cloud platforms such as Amazon Web Services (AWS), Microsoft Azure, and Google Cloud is essential for implementing AI-powered cybersecurity tools in cloud-native environments.

Virtualization technologies like Docker and Kubernetes are also important, as they allow cybersecurity teams to deploy and manage AI-driven tools in containerized environments. This knowledge is critical for protecting cloud-based AI models and ensuring their integrity and confidentiality.

16.3 Career Paths and Opportunities in AI Cybersecurity

The growing demand for AI in cybersecurity has led to the emergence of new career opportunities and specializations. Here are some potential career paths for those looking to combine AI and cybersecurity expertise:

1. AI Cybersecurity Analyst

An AI cybersecurity analyst uses machine learning algorithms to analyze network traffic, identify threats, and respond to incidents. This role requires professionals to continuously monitor systems for anomalies, leveraging AI-driven tools to detect unusual patterns and potential security breaches in real-time. AI cybersecurity analysts often work closely with security operations centers (SOCs) and incident response teams to investigate and mitigate threats.

2. AI Security Engineer

AI security engineers design, develop, and implement AI-based security systems. This role requires a deep understanding of both cybersecurity and AI technologies. Professionals in this field work on creating algorithms that can automatically identify threats, deploy patches, and protect networks without human intervention. They are also responsible for improving the efficiency and effectiveness of these AI-driven solutions.

3. Data Scientist for Cybersecurity

A data scientist specializing in cybersecurity uses AI and data analytics techniques to analyze security data, build predictive models, and provide insights into emerging threats. They work with large datasets, leveraging machine learning algorithms to detect patterns of behavior that could indicate a potential security breach. Data scientists play a crucial role in making sense of vast amounts of security data and helping organizations stay ahead of cybercriminals.

4. Cybersecurity Researcher

Cybersecurity researchers who specialize in AI explore novel ways to use AI to defend against cyber threats. They work on developing new algorithms, AI models, and security protocols to address emerging threats and vulnerabilities. Researchers often work in academic or corporate settings, publishing papers or reports that contribute to the field's knowledge base.

5. Chief AI Security Officer (CAISO)

A Chief AI Security Officer (CAISO) is a senior executive responsible for overseeing the integration of AI technologies into an organization's cybersecurity strategy. The CAISO ensures that AI-powered security tools are aligned with business goals and risk management strategies. This role requires a combination of technical knowledge and leadership skills, as the CAISO is responsible for coordinating efforts across various departments and managing teams of AI and cybersecurity professionals.

6. Penetration Tester (AI-Focused)

Penetration testers with a focus on AI security assess the effectiveness of AI-driven security tools by simulating cyberattacks. Their role involves exploiting vulnerabilities in AI-based systems, ensuring that these tools can withstand sophisticated attacks. This role requires knowledge of both AI and ethical hacking practices to evaluate how well AI security systems can defend against adversarial threats.

16.4 Building Your AI Cybersecurity Portfolio

Building a compelling portfolio is essential for professionals seeking to demonstrate their expertise in AI-driven cybersecurity. Here are key steps for crafting an impactful portfolio:

1. Real-World Projects

Engaging in practical, real-world projects allows professionals to showcase their AI and cybersecurity skills. This could involve developing machine learning models for threat detection, creating an automated incident response system, or building AI-powered phishing detection tools. Documenting these projects with detailed explanations, code samples, and results can make your portfolio stand out to potential employers.

2. Open-Source Contributions

Contributing to open-source AI and cybersecurity projects is a great way to gain experience and show your commitment to continuous learning. Platforms like GitHub offer countless AI-driven security projects that you can participate in. By contributing to these projects, you enhance your technical skills and build a reputation within the community.

3. Certifications and Online Courses

Completing relevant certifications and online courses demonstrates your commitment to mastering the latest AI and cybersecurity techniques. Certifications like the Certified Ethical Hacker (CEH), AWS Certified Security Specialty, or the CompTIA Security+ provide a foundation in cybersecurity, while courses like Coursera's AI for Cybersecurity can deepen your understanding of AI technologies in this context.

4. Blog and Research

Publishing your research, writing blog posts, or creating videos about AI and cybersecurity topics can help you establish yourself as a thought leader in the field. Whether you are discussing new AI algorithms for threat detection, sharing your experience with AI-based security tools, or explaining how AI is transforming the cybersecurity landscape, content creation is a powerful way to demonstrate expertise.

16.5 Certifications and Training Programs in AI and Cybersecurity

Several certifications and training programs are specifically designed to equip professionals with the skills needed for AI-driven cybersecurity roles. These programs help individuals build a strong foundation in both cybersecurity and AI, enhancing their qualifications and marketability.

1. Certified Information Systems Security Professional (CISSP)

CISSP is one of the most recognized certifications in cybersecurity. While not AI-specific, CISSP provides the foundational knowledge needed to understand cybersecurity principles that are essential when integrating AI into security strategies.

2. Certified Ethical Hacker (CEH)

CEH focuses on ethical hacking techniques, helping professionals understand how attackers use AI and other technologies to compromise systems. This certification covers threat analysis, penetration testing, and security auditing, skills crucial for AI-focused cybersecurity roles.

3. CompTIA Security+

CompTIA Security+ is a fundamental cybersecurity certification, and while not AI-focused, it covers essential security topics that are relevant when working with AI-based security tools, such as threat management, risk assessment, and identity management.

4. AI for Cybersecurity (Coursera)

This course, offered by IBM on Coursera, teaches professionals how to apply AI techniques for threat detection, risk assessment, and incident response. It covers machine learning, anomaly detection, and neural networks in the context of cybersecurity.

5. AWS Certified Security Specialty

This certification focuses on security best practices for cloud environments, including AI-based security solutions. AWS's cloud security tools, many of which leverage AI, are critical for professionals working in cloud-based cybersecurity roles.

16.6 The Role of AI in Shaping the Future of Cybersecurity Careers

AI is driving a transformation in the cybersecurity job market, changing how professionals approach security and what skills they need. By automating tasks such as threat detection, incident response, and malware analysis, AI frees cybersecurity professionals to focus on higher-level strategy and decision-making. As AI continues to evolve, its impact on the cybersecurity workforce will only grow.

In the future, AI expertise will be a critical differentiator in the cybersecurity workforce. Professionals with both AI and cybersecurity knowledge will have an edge as AI-powered security solutions become integral to defense strategies. Cybersecurity roles will increasingly focus on integrating and managing AI technologies, creating new opportunities for professionals to lead the charge in the next generation of cyber defense.

16.7 How AI Will Transform Job Roles in Cyber Defense

AI will significantly alter job roles in cyber defense by automating routine tasks and enhancing human capabilities. Security analysts and engineers will use AI tools to speed up the detection and mitigation of threats. In some cases, AI will completely replace roles focused on repetitive tasks, like network traffic analysis or log monitoring.

However, AI will not eliminate the need for human oversight. Professionals will continue interpreting AI findings, investigating complex incidents, and developing new strategies for handling advanced threats. As AI evolves, the future cyber defense workforce will include many hybrid roles combining AI, data science, and cybersecurity expertise.

Professionals who stay ahead of AI trends will be well-positioned to adapt to these evolving job roles and capitalize on AI's new opportunities to the cybersecurity industry.

Appendices

A. Glossary of Key Terms

Adversarial AI

A technique used by cybercriminals to manipulate or deceive AI systems. Adversarial AI can trick machine learning models into making inaccurate predictions or classifications, which can undermine security systems.

Adversarial Machine Learning

A subfield of machine learning focused on understanding and defending against attacks that manipulate the learning process itself. It explores methods for making machine learning systems more robust against adversarial inputs.

AI-Driven Security Tools

Software and systems that leverage AI and machine learning to perform tasks such as threat detection, vulnerability assessment, and incident response. These tools continuously learn and adapt to emerging threats.

Artificial Intelligence (AI)

The simulation of human intelligence processes by machines, particularly computer systems. AI includes learning, reasoning, and self-correction capabilities. In cybersecurity, AI detects threats, predicts vulnerabilities, and automates security processes.

Artificial Neural Network (ANN)

A computational model inspired by the way the human brain works. ANNs are used in AI to recognize patterns and make decisions and are integral in deep learning models for cybersecurity tasks like malware detection and threat classification.

Behavioral Analytics

The use of machine learning to analyze patterns of user behavior and detect anomalies that may indicate a security threat. This is particularly useful in identifying insider threats or compromised user accounts.

Botnet

A network of infected devices controlled by a cybercriminal to carry out malicious activities, such as launching Distributed Denial of Service (DDoS) attacks or stealing data. AI can help detect botnets by analyzing network traffic for signs of abnormal behavior.

Cloud Security

The practice of protecting data, applications, and systems in cloud environments from cyber threats. AI plays a significant role in cloud security by identifying vulnerabilities, detecting attacks, and automating security responses.

Cyber Threat Hunting

The proactive search for potential threats within a network or system. Threat hunters use AI tools to analyze data and identify signs of malicious activity before they can cause harm.

Cybersecurity

The practice of protecting systems, networks, and programs from digital attacks. It involves a range of strategies, tools, and policies aimed at defending against unauthorized access, data breaches, and cyberattacks.

Cybersecurity Mesh Architecture (CSMA)

A flexible, modular security approach that allows organizations to protect all their digital assets, regardless of their location. AI enhances CSMA by dynamically adapting security measures based on real-time data and emerging threats.

Data Science

A multidisciplinary field that uses scientific methods, algorithms, and systems to extract insights from structured and unstructured data. In cybersecurity, data science is used to analyze large datasets, identify trends, and detect threats.

Deep Learning (DL)

A subset of machine learning that utilizes neural networks with multiple layers to analyze and interpret data. Deep learning is particularly effective in areas such as image recognition, speech recognition, and detecting sophisticated cyber threats like malware.

Encryption

The process of converting data into a code to prevent unauthorized access. AI tools can improve encryption techniques by predicting and protecting against vulnerabilities before they can be exploited.

Ethical AI

The development and deployment of AI systems in a way that ensures fairness, transparency, and accountability, while minimizing bias. Ethical AI is critical in cybersecurity to avoid discrimination and to protect privacy.

False Positive

A situation where a security system mistakenly identifies a legitimate action as malicious or suspicious. Minimizing false positives is important in AI-driven cybersecurity systems to ensure efficiency and accuracy.

Incident Response

The process of identifying, investigating, and responding to cybersecurity incidents. AI helps automate incident response by analyzing data in real-time and providing recommendations for containment and mitigation.

Intrusion Detection System (IDS)

A system designed to detect unauthorized access to a network or system. IDS relies on predefined patterns or machine learning algorithms to identify malicious activity and potential breaches.

Intrusion Prevention System (IPS)

A security system that detects and prevents identified threats by taking immediate action, such as blocking malicious traffic. AI can enhance IPS by automatically adapting to new attack techniques and responding in real-time.

Machine Learning (ML)

A subset of AI enables systems to learn from data and improve their performance without being explicitly programmed. In cybersecurity, ML algorithms are commonly used for tasks like anomaly detection, intrusion detection, and threat prediction.

Malware

Software designed to disrupt, damage, or gain unauthorized access to a computer system. AI is used in cybersecurity to detect and classify new types of malware based on patterns and behaviors.

Natural Language Processing (NLP)

A field of AI focused on enabling machines to understand, interpret, and respond to human language. NLP is used in cybersecurity for tasks like detecting phishing emails, analyzing chat logs for threats, and automating responses to security incidents.

Phishing

A form of social engineering in which cybercriminals trick individuals into revealing personal information or credentials. AI is increasingly used to detect phishing attempts by analyzing email patterns, language, and sender behavior.

Penetration Testing (Pen Testing)

The process of testing a computer system, network, or web application to identify vulnerabilities that attackers could exploit. Penetration testers often use AI tools to simulate real-world cyberattacks and assess system defenses.

Ransomware

A type of malicious software that encrypts a victim's data and demands a ransom in exchange for the decryption key. AI-driven systems can identify ransomware attacks by analyzing abnormal behavior patterns in files and systems.

Security Automation

AI and machine learning are used to automate routine security tasks such as vulnerability scanning, incident response, and patch management. This reduces the need for manual intervention and accelerates response times.

Security Information and Event Management (SIEM)

A system that collects and analyzes security data from various sources to provide real-time insights into security events and potential threats. AI can be integrated into SIEM platforms to automate threat detection and response.

Threat Intelligence

Information about existing or emerging cyber threats, including data on potential attackers, attack techniques, and vulnerabilities. Threat intelligence is essential for developing proactive security measures and for detecting and responding to cyberattacks.

Threat Landscape

The evolving state of cyber threats, including the types of threats, attack methods, and targets. AI monitors and predicts changes in the threat landscape to provide timely defenses.

Zero-Day Attack

A type of cyberattack that exploits a previously unknown vulnerability in software or hardware. AI can help detect zero-day attacks by analyzing system behavior and identifying anomalies that could indicate an attack.

Zero-Day Exploit

A method used by attackers to exploit a previously unknown vulnerability in software or hardware, often before a patch or fix is available. AI can assist in detecting these exploits by identifying unusual behavior in applications or systems.

B. Additional Resources for Learning AI in Cybersecurity

Books on AI and Cybersecurity

"Artificial Intelligence in Cybersecurity" by Leslie F. Sikos

This book delves into the role of AI in cybersecurity, providing a comprehensive guide to the integration of AI technologies with traditional security measures.

"Machine Learning for Cybersecurity" by Josh More

A practical guide to leveraging machine learning for various cybersecurity applications, including fraud detection, malware analysis, and intrusion prevention.

"Cybersecurity and Artificial Intelligence: Theories, Techniques, and Tools" by Antonios Chatzigiannakis and Stathes Hadjiefthymiades

This book provides theoretical foundations along with practical techniques on how AI can be used for cybersecurity solutions.

Online Courses and Certifications

Coursera: AI for Cybersecurity Specialization

Offered by the University of Colorado, this program explores how AI can be used for detecting threats and securing IT infrastructures.

Udemy: Machine Learning for Cybersecurity

A beginner-to-intermediate level course teaches how to apply machine learning techniques to enhance cybersecurity.

edX: Artificial Intelligence for Cybersecurity

A course offered by Stanford University that focuses on using AI techniques to detect and mitigate cybersecurity threats.

Cybrary: Artificial Intelligence in Cybersecurity

Cybrary's cybersecurity certification courses, including AI-based topics in security, are beneficial for building real-world AI applications in the field.

AI and Cybersecurity Podcasts

"The AI in Cybersecurity Podcast"

Hosted by top cybersecurity professionals, this podcast delves into the latest advancements in AI-driven cybersecurity technologies and real-world applications.

"Darknet Diaries"

While primarily focused on real-life hacking stories, Darknet Diaries occasionally explores the intersection of AI and cybersecurity, including how adversaries use AI for cybercrime.

"CyberWire Daily Podcast"

This podcast covers the latest cybersecurity news, with frequent discussions on AI's role in modern cyber defense strategies.

"Cybersecurity AI Show"

A show that specifically focuses on how AI is being integrated into cybersecurity, discussing tools, technologies, and the ethics of AI usage.

AI Cybersecurity Blogs and Websites

AI in Cybersecurity by Darktrace

Darktrace's website regularly publishes blog posts and case studies that show how their AI technology is applied to detect and defend against advanced cybersecurity threats.

Artificial Intelligence Cybersecurity by IBM

IBM's AI and cybersecurity division shares insights on AI-driven threat detection, vulnerability management, and real-time security automation.

McAfee AI Blog

McAfee's blog offers thought leadership on integrating AI into cybersecurity tools, including malware detection, fraud prevention, and more.

AI for Cybersecurity by Cisco

Cisco's AI section features articles on how their AI-powered solutions can be used to protect against evolving threats, with an emphasis on network security.

AI and Cybersecurity Research Papers

"Artificial Intelligence for Cybersecurity: The New Frontier" – Published in *IEEE Access*

This research paper discusses how AI and machine learning models can assist in defending against a wide range of cyberattacks, such as network intrusions, phishing, and malware.

"AI-Based Cybersecurity: Challenges and Solutions" – Published in *SpringerLink*

This paper thoroughly analyzes the challenges organizations face when implementing AI-driven cybersecurity solutions and offers recommendations for overcoming them.

"The Role of Machine Learning in Cyber Defense" – Published in *Journal of Cybersecurity*

A research paper focusing on how machine learning can be utilized for threat intelligence and automated defense mechanisms in modern security operations.

Conferences and Webinars

Black Hat USA

An annual conference where the latest research and developments in cybersecurity are presented. Many sessions focus on AI and its applications in cybersecurity.

RSA Conference

A global cybersecurity conference that includes sessions on artificial intelligence, machine learning, and their use in the fight against cybercrime.

DEF CON

DEF CON features numerous talks on the intersection of AI and cybersecurity, with many experts in the field presenting their latest research and practical applications.

AI in Cybersecurity Webinars by SANS Institute

SANS Institute frequently hosts free and paid webinars that explore how to use AI in cybersecurity defense strategies.

AI and Cybersecurity Research Institutions and Think Tanks

The AI Cybersecurity Research Institute

This think tank focuses on developing cutting-edge research on AI in cybersecurity and offering resources for professionals looking to understand and implement AI security solutions.

MIT Artificial Intelligence and Cybersecurity Lab

MIT's lab conducts groundbreaking research on AI-driven cybersecurity solutions, offering both research papers and industry insights.

The Center for Security and Emerging Technologies (CSET)

A think tank that investigates how emerging technologies, including AI, can be used for national security and cyber defense. CSET publishes research reports and policy recommendations.

Gartner AI in Cybersecurity Reports

Gartner publishes detailed reports that evaluate the effectiveness of AI-powered cybersecurity technologies and provide market analysis.

Online Communities and Forums

AI and Cybersecurity Subreddit (r/CybersecurityAI)

A community of cybersecurity professionals who share the latest trends, research, and discussions around AI in cybersecurity.

Stack Overflow: AI in Cybersecurity Discussions

Stack Overflow is an invaluable resource for asking questions and finding technical discussions on AI tools used for cybersecurity.

Cybersecurity and AI LinkedIn Groups

Several LinkedIn groups focus on discussions related to AI in cybersecurity, offering networking opportunities, webinars, and industry insights.

AI and Cybersecurity Discord Channel

A Discord community where AI professionals and cybersecurity experts collaborate to solve technical challenges and share resources.

AI Tools and Software for Practice

TensorFlow by Google

An open-source machine learning library widely used for implementing AI models in various domains, including cybersecurity. It provides resources to help implement algorithms that can be used in threat detection and response.

PyTorch

PyTorch is another popular deep learning library to develop cybersecurity application AI models. It is known for its flexibility and use in both academic research and industry applications.

OpenAI GPT-3

OpenAI's GPT-3 can be utilized to develop intelligent systems for natural language processing tasks, including phishing detection, spam filtering, and threat intelligence.

Keras

A Python-based neural network library that runs on top of TensorFlow, making it easier to create deep learning models for applications such as malware detection.

AI Cybersecurity Vendor Websites

CrowdStrike

CrowdStrike's website offers whitepapers, case studies, and blogs showcasing how AI is integrated into its threat detection and endpoint protection solutions.

Darktrace

Darktrace specializes in AI for cybersecurity, offering resources, webinars, and case studies that demonstrate their AI's ability to autonomously detect and respond to cyber threats.

Cylance

Cylance's AI-driven security products are designed to prevent threats before they occur. Their website provides resources on their AI technology and how it improves threat detection and prevention.

IBM Security

IBM Security offers a wide range of AI-powered cybersecurity solutions. Their website includes case studies, whitepapers, and technical documentation on using AI in cybersecurity.

C. References

The following is a comprehensive list of references, including books, academic papers, white papers, industry reports, and websites that were consulted and cited throughout this book. These resources are intended to guide readers who wish to explore specific topics further, providing additional depth and context for key concepts discussed.

Books:

1. Anderson, R. (2020). *Security Engineering: A Guide to Building Dependable Distributed Systems*. Wiley.
2. Bishop, M. (2003). *Computer Security: Art and Science*. Addison-Wesley.
3. Chen, Z., & Li, H. (2018). *Artificial Intelligence for Cybersecurity: Tools and Techniques*. CRC Press.
4. Kaspersky Lab (2019). *AI for Cybersecurity: Understanding AI and Machine Learning*. Kaspersky Labs.
5. Ng, A. (2016). *Machine Learning Yearning*. deeplearning.ai.
6. Stallings, W. (2017). *Cryptography and Network Security: Principles and Practice*. Pearson.

Research Papers:

1. Bostrom, N., & Yudkowsky, E. (2014). *The Ethics of Artificial Intelligence*. Cambridge Handbook of Artificial Intelligence.
2. He, K., Zhang, X., Ren, S., & Sun, J. (2016). *Deep Residual Learning for Image Recognition*. IEEE Conference on Computer Vision and Pattern Recognition.
3. Moustafa, N., & Slay, J. (2017). *A Survey of Intrusion Detection Systems using Machine Learning*. International Journal of Computer Applications.
4. Papernot, N., McDaniel, P., & Goodfellow, I. (2016). *Transferability in Machine Learning*. Proceedings of the 33rd International Conference on Machine Learning (ICML).

Industry Reports:

1. CrowdStrike. (2021). *Global Threat Report: AI-Powered Cybersecurity*. Retrieved from https://www.crowdstrike.com.
2. IBM Security. (2020). *The Cost of a Data Breach Report*. IBM. Retrieved from https://www.ibm.com/security/data-breach.
3. McAfee. (2020). *The State of Cybersecurity in the AI Era*. McAfee Labs.
4. MIT Technology Review. (2020). *AI and the Future of Cybersecurity*. MIT Technology Review.

White Papers:

1. Darktrace. (2021). *The Role of AI in Cyber Defense*. Darktrace Inc. Retrieved from https://www.darktrace.com.
2. Fortinet. (2019). *Next-Generation AI for Cybersecurity*. Fortinet. Retrieved from https://www.fortinet.com.
3. Palo Alto Networks. (2021). *AI for Threat Detection and Prevention*. Palo Alto Networks. Retrieved from https://www.paloaltonetworks.com.

Websites:

1. *Artificial Intelligence and Cybersecurity: What You Need to Know*. (2021). AI Cybersecurity News. Retrieved from https://www.aicybersecuritynews.com.
2. *National Institute of Standards and Technology (NIST)*. (2021). Cybersecurity Framework. Retrieved from https://www.nist.gov/cybersecurity.
3. *OpenAI*. (2021). *Machine Learning Models for Cybersecurity*. Retrieved from https://www.openai.com.
4. *Stanford AI Research*. (2020). *Applications of AI in Cybersecurity*. Retrieved from https://ai.stanford.edu.

Standards and Frameworks:

1. National Institute of Standards and Technology (NIST) (2018). *NIST Cybersecurity Framework*. NIST. Retrieved from https://www.nist.gov/cyberframework.
2. ISO/IEC 27001:2013. *Information Security Management Systems*. International Organization for Standardization (ISO).
3. ITIL (2019). *Information Technology Infrastructure Library: Service Management Framework*. Axelos.

Conferences and Symposiums:

1. IEEE Symposium on Security and Privacy (2019). *AI and Cybersecurity: Techniques and Technologies*. IEEE.
2. RSA Conference (2021). *Cybersecurity AI Trends and Challenges*. RSA Conference, San Francisco, USA.
3. Black Hat USA (2020). *AI for Threat Detection: Challenges and Innovations*. Black Hat.

Technical Blogs and Articles:

1. Caldera, R. (2020). *How AI is Transforming the Cybersecurity Landscape*. Dark Reading. Retrieved from https://www.darkreading.com.
2. Johnson, M. (2021). *AI and Cybersecurity: Current Trends and Future Prospects*. Wired. Retrieved from https://www.wired.com.
3. Liu, L. (2021). *Using Machine Learning to Detect Cyber Attacks*. Medium. Retrieved from https://medium.com.

Online Courses and Certifications:

1. Coursera. (2020). *AI for Cybersecurity Specialization*. Coursera. Retrieved from https://www.coursera.org.
2. edX. (2021). *Artificial Intelligence for Cybersecurity Professionals*. edX. Retrieved from https://www.edx.org.

3. Stanford University. (2021). *AI and Machine Learning for Cybersecurity*. Stanford University Online.

AI Cybersecurity Certifications

The growing intersection of artificial intelligence (AI) and cybersecurity has led to an increase in specialized certifications that can help professionals stay ahead in the field. These certifications focus on equipping individuals with the knowledge and skills necessary to integrate AI into cybersecurity practices, ensuring that organizations can combat the ever-evolving threat landscape. Below is a list of certifications that help professionals enhance their knowledge and career prospects in this domain.

1. Certified AI Cybersecurity Professional (AICP)

The AICP certification is designed for professionals who wish to specialize in AI-driven cybersecurity technologies. The certification program includes:

- **AI for Threat Detection**: How AI can be leveraged to detect and respond to cybersecurity threats.
- **Machine Learning in Security**: Understanding the application of machine learning algorithms in anomaly detection, malware analysis, and intrusion detection systems (IDS).
- **AI Security Principles**: Learning the security implications of AI, including privacy, fairness, and ethical concerns.

This certification is ideal for cybersecurity professionals seeking to expand their knowledge of AI technologies and their integration into cybersecurity practices.

2. Certified Information Systems Security Professional (CISSP) with AI Specialization

The CISSP certification, offered by (ISC)², is one of the most widely recognized cybersecurity certifications. With an AI specialization, this certification allows professionals to deepen their understanding of how AI can enhance information security practices.

- **Security Architecture**: Learning how AI can be embedded into security systems, from designing to securing systems.
- **AI-Driven Risk Management**: Incorporating AI tools to manage cybersecurity risks and protect data.
- **Ethical AI in Security**: Understanding the ethical issues involved in deploying AI for cybersecurity.

3. Certified Ethical Hacker (CEH) with AI Integration

The CEH certification focuses on ethical hacking and penetration testing techniques, including the use of AI in these areas. AI is particularly useful in automating vulnerability scanning, exploiting weaknesses, and identifying zero-day threats.

- **AI for Vulnerability Scanning**: Automating vulnerability discovery using AI-powered tools.
- **AI-Powered Pen Testing**: Using machine learning models to simulate attacks and test defenses.
- **AI in Malware Analysis**: Leveraging AI for identifying and analyzing new malware threats.

4. GIAC Security Essentials (GSEC)

The Global Information Assurance Certification (GIAC) offers the GSEC certification as an entry-level credential that includes knowledge of how AI technologies are applied in basic cybersecurity practices. It provides an introduction to AI concepts within the context of protecting information and systems.

- **Foundational AI Security Concepts**: An introduction to AI and its role in cybersecurity.
- **AI in Network Defense**: Understanding how AI can be used to monitor and secure network traffic.

5. CompTIA Security+ with AI Integration

The CompTIA Security+ certification is an industry-standard credential for cybersecurity professionals. A growing focus on AI integration has led to updates in the curriculum that include how AI can be applied to basic cybersecurity functions such as intrusion detection, encryption, and risk management.

- **AI in Risk Management**: Applying AI to evaluate and mitigate cybersecurity risks.
- **AI for Security Automation**: Using AI for automating responses to security events and incidents.

6. Certified Artificial Intelligence Security Specialist (CAISS)

The CAISS certification is designed for professionals who want to specialize in using AI to strengthen security operations and detect emerging cyber threats. The certification focuses on:

- **AI-Based Threat Detection**: Learning how to utilize machine learning and deep learning models to detect, identify, and mitigate cyber threats in real-time.
- **Secure AI Integration**: Understanding how to integrate AI models securely into an organization's existing cybersecurity infrastructure.

- **Threat Intelligence**: Leveraging AI for actionable threat intelligence that improves response times and proactively mitigates risks.

This certification is ideal for cybersecurity professionals who aim to leverage AI to enhance threat detection and response capabilities.

7. Certified Cloud Security Professional (CCSP) with AI Specialization

The CCSP certification, offered by $(ISC)^2$, focuses on cloud security principles, best practices, and governance, including the integration of AI into cloud environments. With an AI specialization, the certification delves into:

- **AI in Cloud Security**: Understanding how AI models can be applied to secure cloud environments by detecting vulnerabilities, managing access controls, and mitigating risks.
- **AI in Data Encryption**: Learning how AI-powered encryption models can provide dynamic protection against data breaches in cloud infrastructure.
- **Cloud-based AI Security Tools**: Integrating AI-powered security tools to monitor cloud networks for potential threats.

The CCSP certification with an AI focus is an excellent choice for professionals working in cloud security, particularly those looking to expand their expertise in AI-driven solutions.

8. Certified Information Security Manager (CISM) with AI Integration

ISACA offers the CISM certification, a globally recognized credential for individuals focusing on managing and overseeing information security programs. With AI integration, this certification covers the following:

- **AI for Risk Management**: Using AI to assess and manage cybersecurity risks by analyzing vast amounts of data and detecting emerging threats.
- **Security Governance and AI**: Understanding how AI impacts the governance of information security frameworks and helps organizations align with security policies.
- **Incident Response with AI**: Implementing AI tools for automated incident response to mitigate cyberattacks quickly and efficiently.

The CISM certification with an AI focus is ideal for cybersecurity managers who need to incorporate AI-driven tools into their governance and risk management strategies.

9. Certified Information Systems Auditor (CISA) with AI Focus

The CISA certification is widely recognized for its focus on auditing, control, and assurance of information systems. With an AI focus, the certification addresses the following:

- **Auditing AI Systems**: Learning how to audit AI-driven security systems for efficiency, security, and compliance.
- **AI-Based Threat Detection in Auditing**: Using AI tools to identify anomalies and potential breaches during system audits.
- **AI-Driven Risk Assessments**: Conducting automated risk assessments using AI to identify potential threats and vulnerabilities.

This certification is suitable for professionals interested in auditing and securing AI-based systems in cybersecurity operations.

10. CompTIA Advanced Security Practitioner (CASP+) with AI Integration

CompTIA's CASP+ is an advanced certification for experienced security practitioners. With AI integration, the certification includes:

- **AI for Security Operations**: Implementing AI tools for enhanced security monitoring and automated defense mechanisms.
- **AI and Incident Management**: Leveraging AI for detecting incidents early and responding to them in real-time.
- **Adversarial AI in Cybersecurity**: Understanding how adversarial AI can be used to counterattack or trick traditional security systems and how to defend against it.

CASP+ is ideal for senior cybersecurity professionals who need advanced skills in managing AI-driven security infrastructures.

11. Artificial Intelligence in Cybersecurity Certification (AISEC)

The AISEC certification focuses entirely on applying AI and machine learning techniques to cybersecurity challenges. The program includes:

- **AI in Malware Detection**: Using AI to detect and analyze new malware strains.
- **Threat Prediction with AI**: Employing predictive AI models to forecast potential cybersecurity threats.
- **AI for Data Privacy**: Learning how AI can be applied to ensure compliance with data privacy regulations such as GDPR.

This certification is suited for professionals who specialize in the development and application of AI-based solutions in cybersecurity.

12. Cisco Certified CyberOps Associate (CCCA) with AI Integration

The CCCA certification from Cisco focuses on security operations and is part of Cisco's CyberOps certification track. With AI integration, the certification addresses:

- **AI for Security Automation**: Understanding how to integrate AI models into security operations to automate response workflows and speed up the detection and mitigation of threats.
- **AI in Network Security**: Leveraging AI for continuous monitoring and securing network traffic from cyber threats.
- **Behavioral Analytics with AI**: Using AI to analyze network behavior and detect deviations that could indicate a cybersecurity threat.

The CCCA with AI focus is an excellent choice for professionals working in security operations and network defense.

www.ingramcontent.com/pod-product-compliance
Lightning Source LLC
LaVergne TN
LVHW051233050326
832903LV00028B/2379